THE TRAMWAYS
OF
LYTHAM ST ANNES

by
P.H. Abell, J.A. Garnham and I. McLoughlin

THE OAKWOOD PRESS

© Oakwood Press, P.H. Abell, J.A. Garnham and I. McLoughlin

British Library Cataloguing in Publication Data
A Record for this book is available from the British Library
ISBN 0 85361 475 X

Typeset by Oakwood Graphics.

Printed by Alpha Print (Oxford) Ltd, Witney, Oxon

Dedicated to Jim Ingham, colleague, friend and Chairman of the Fylde Tramway Society 1976-1980.

Above: Lytham gas tram No.4, a small car of the original series, as tested in Paris in 1896.
IM Collection

Opposite: Tram No.8 at the Cottage Hospital terminus in Lytham in Company days.
IM Collection

Front Cover: No.6 shortly after entering service. *JG Collection*

Title page: Lytham St Annes Corporation Transport coat of arms. *G.S. Palmer*

Published by
The Oakwood Press
P.O. Box 122, Headington, Oxford

Contents

Lytham St Annes Tramway

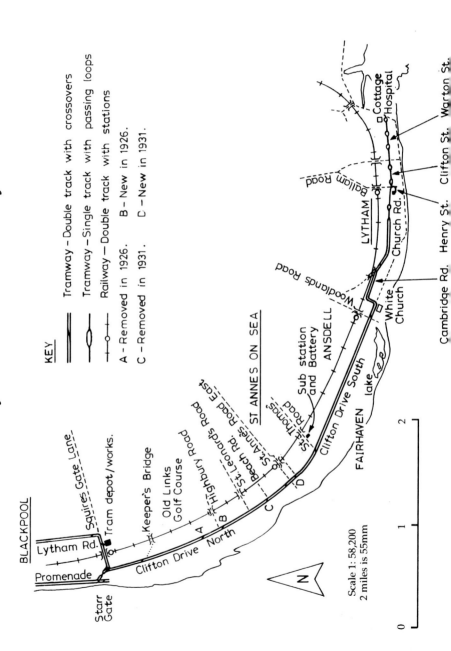

KEY

Tramway – Double track with crossovers
Tramway – Single track with passing loops
Railway – Double track with stations

A – Removed in 1926.   B – New in 1926.
C – Removed in 1931.   D – New in 1931.

BLACKPOOL
Starr Gate
Promenade
Lytham Rd.
Squires Gate Lane
Tram depot/works.
Keeper's Bridge
Old Links Golf Course
Highbury Road
St. Leonards Road
Beech Rd.
St. Annes Road East
St. Annes Rd.
St. Thomas' Road
ST ANNES ON SEA
Clifton Drive North
Sub station and Battery
ANSDELL
Woodlands Road
Clifton Drive South
FAIRHAVEN
lake
White Church
Church Rd.
LYTHAM
Ballam Road
Cottage Hospital
Cambridge Rd.   Henry St.   Clifton St.   Warton St.

N

Scale 1: 58,200
2 miles is 55mm

0   1   2

Introduction

The districts of Lytham and St Annes have always had a character distinctive from that of their northern neighbour on the Fylde Coast, Blackpool.

This is the story of a part of that distinctive character: the tramway history of the twin towns diverged from that of Blackpool from the start, with the courageous decision to employ gas trams, powered by the internal-combustion engine, which was to come to dominate passenger transport in the 20th century after the false dawn of the Edwardian tramway boom.

A political decision in the 1930s turned Lytham St Annes (less precisely named Fylde Borough after local government reorganisation in 1974) into a district of the Fylde Coast set apart from Blackpool, Cleveleys and Fleetwood by not having trams, and people visited it less. Perhaps if the councillors of the time had seen the recent estimate that visitors bring £438 million into Blackpool each year their decision might have been different.

Will trams ever return to St Annes and Lytham? As tramway enthusiasts we would like to see this very much, but as observers of the social scene we must point out that the heyday of tramways was a time when aspirants to middle-class status felt that their position in society was demonstrated by the employment of domestic servants, rather than the possession of a carefully-marketed motor car for personal transport. Thus both masters and servants swelled the ranks of potential tram passengers. A new tramway system would have to be very attractive to win passengers from their own cars: some form of electric light railway has been suggested for the under-used line between Blackpool South Shore, St Annes, Lytham and Kirkham, but an extension to Preston for employment and shopping might be necessary to produce a viable scheme.

Meanwhile there is a twist in the tale of this story with the recent takeover of Blue Buses (successors of Lytham St Annes Borough Tramways and Fylde Borough Transport) by Blackpool Transport Services Limited, who as operators of the Blackpool tramway are actively involved in developing new tram designs. Hopefully in years to come there will be another tramway in Lytham and St Annes to be chronicled by our successors.

An early view of No.23 with one of the 1-20 series behind, at St Annes Square.

IM Collection

Map of Through Running by Lytham St Annes Trams over Blackpool Corporation Tracks July 1896-July 1905

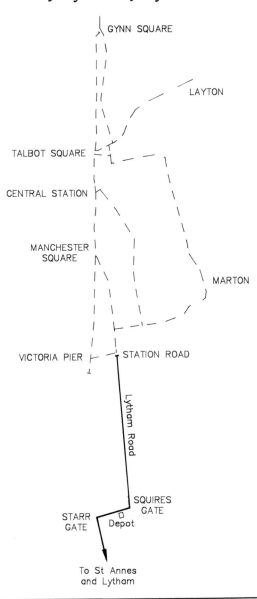

GYNN SQUARE

LAYTON

TALBOT SQUARE

CENTRAL STATION

MANCHESTER SQUARE

MARTON

VICTORIA PIER

STATION ROAD

Lytham Road

SQUIRES GATE

STARR GATE

Depot

To St Annes and Lytham

Chapter One

The Gas Tramway 1896-1903

Lytham was an established settlement when it was mentioned in the Domesday Book in 1086, and in the Middle Ages a priory near the site of Lytham Hall improved the area until the Dissolution of the Monasteries. After various secular owners the Manor of Lytham was bought for £4,300 in 1606 by Cuthbert Clifton of Westby, starting an association with the benevolent Clifton family which lasted until 1963. The beginnings of modern Lytham can be dated to the 1770s, when the fashion for sea bathing brought the first visitors to the Fylde. A branch of the Preston and Wyre Railway in 1846 was followed by the Lytham Improvement Act the following year, and for much of the 19th century Lytham was a bigger centre than Blackpool.

On the other hand the establishment of St Annes as a district can be dated to the 1870s: in 1872 Lady Eleanor Cecily Clifton promoted the building of St Anne's Parish Church, whilst two years later a Rossendale cotton magnate, Elijah Hargreaves, promoted the St Annes Land and Building Company to develop a square mile of Clifton land, starting with the St Annes Hotel in 1875. The good train service provided to Manchester (in particular) by the Lancashire & Yorkshire Railway enabled the town to develop as a residential area for Lancashire businessmen as well as a holiday resort. The Fairhaven Estate Company was formed in 1895, and created a new suburb out of the sandhills between St Annes and Lytham.

The boom of the 1890s brought proposals for a tramway to link Lytham and St Annes with the growing prosperity of Blackpool, incorporated as a borough in 1876 and crowned by the completion of the Tower in 1894. Horse tramways had been a growing urban phenomenon in Britain since the 1860s, though their fares tended to be high for working men, horses were expensive to operate and steep gradients brought problems which often prompted the adoption of steam tramways in hilly towns in the 1880s. Another possibility occasionally found in hilly districts was the cable tramway (as in San Francisco), but this required massive capital investment to thread the haulage cables under the streets along the whole distance of the routes, and it was made obsolete for new lines by the development of reliable electric tramways.

A pioneer in electric traction, Blackpool had had an electric tramway along the Promenade since 1885, but instead of the overhead wires which were to become so familiar in many towns and cities the electric current was supplied to the cars by means of metal strips in an underground conduit between the rails. This arrangement was always vulnerable to sand and salt spray on the exposed seafront, there were problems maintaining the service and occasionally the trams had to revert to horse traction. The Blackpool St Annes and Lytham Tramways Act permitted operation by horse or mechanical traction, but not by steam or cable. In fact the tramway on to St Annes and Lytham was to turn to gas traction when it commenced operations in 1896.

The section of tramway in Blackpool was constructed by Blackpool

Gas tram No.19 takes a good load of passengers through Market Square in Lytham.

JG Collection

Although not of good quality this is an extremely rare and historic photograph, showing several of the gas trams that were badly damaged after the Lytham Road tram depot was destroyed by strong gales on 27th February, 1903. The large flywheel, underframe, and truck is all that remains of the tram in the foreground. *G.S. Palmer Collection*

Corporation and leased to the Blackpool St Annes and Lytham Tramways Company (incorporated in 1893) for 21 years at an annual rent of £517. A double track ran along Lytham Road from the old South Shore Station (later replaced by South), convenient for, but not physically connected to, the terminus of the Blackpool Corporation trams out along Lytham Road (this line had been opened as a conduit electric tramway in September 1895, and was converted to overhead wires four years later). After just over a mile the track turned right at the end of Lytham Road, leaving Blackpool and running onto Stonyhill Road (now Squires Gate Lane). The remainder of the route was built by the Tramways Company at a cost of £34,000, and was mainly single track with passing loops, crossing the railway then turning left along Clifton Drive to run another two miles to St Annes, opened on Saturday 11th July, 1896, then extended three miles through Fairhaven and Ansdell to Market Square, Lytham, on 21st February, 1897.

There could have been other routes for the gas trams. The Blackpool St Annes and Lytham Tramways Act 1893 authorised the construction of ¼-mile of tramway up St Annes Road East from St Annes Square to St Andrews Road North, but it was not to be commenced without the consent of the local railway companies (the Lancashire & Yorkshire and the London & North Western). This consent was not forthcoming, and the line was dropped from the 1896 Act, which revived the powers for the lines actually built, and also for some additional track in the centre of Lytham which was never laid. A 600-yds-long single line would have turned left from Church Road into Hastings Place and run to Lytham station, returning via the end of Upper Westby Street and Park Street to send cars into Church Road heading back towards St Annes and Blackpool. Another 120 yards of single line along Upper Westby Street would have given a direct connection between Hastings Place and Park Street, avoiding the station.

Meanwhile the operation of the tramway had been leased to the British Gas Traction Company, formed in 1896 to exploit the Luhrig system of gas traction for tramways, already operating at Dessau, 70 miles south-west of Berlin, and improved by Mr P.H. Holt of Crossley Brothers in Manchester. The four-wheel trams were each powered by a two-cylinder Otto gas engine supplied from three reservoirs of coal gas mounted under the tram, rendering unnecessary the provision of electricity by overhead wires or the conduit system. British Gas Traction agreed to work the line for seven years for 4.5d. per car mile run, with a minimum of about 163,000 miles per annum. The cost per mile included the wages of the driver but not the conductor, who was employed by the Tramway Company.

The service at first was sparse, two trams in traffic with a running speed of 9 mph providing a 40 minute service between St Annes and Blackpool South Shore, but by the following year a batch of new trams had increased the fleet to 20. British Gas Traction started operations in Trafford Park in July 1897, and in Neath in August 1899, but serious financial difficulties forced the company into compulsory liquidation by November of that year, having given up operating the Lytham line in 1898.

What went wrong? At this time there had not been the 20th century

One of the larger gas trams (the artist has omitted the engine controls and brakes from the platform).

Frank Dickinson

development along the coast, the total population of St Annes was only around 7,000, and there were said to be only 92 houses on or near the track from South Shore station to Ansdell - most of the district being bare sandhills. The gas trams themselves were charged with gas twice on the journey through to Lytham (at Squires Gate corner and then in Cambridge Road, Ansdell), and their slow progress over the railway bridges at South Shore and Squires Gate reputedly had to be helped by passengers pushing on occasions. Since it was necessary to change cars onto a Blackpool tram at South Shore station in any case, it is not difficult to imagine that the average person in Lytham might try the new trams for one trip to Blackpool then return to the comfort of the trains running along the parallel railway line straight into Blackpool Central station. In contrast such a novelty as the gas trams might well appeal to visitors to the Fylde on a fine day: if they were used to the clatter of a typical weaving shed they would not be troubled too much by the popping of a gas engine. Hence contemporary reports contrast 78,000 passengers in the winter six months of 1896-7 with 200,000 in the summer six months of 1897, and half a million the following summer, when the company was unable to cope with peak traffic. Six trams were sufficient for the winter, but 14 could be out in the summer to give a 10 minute service.

The perception of electric tramways locally was radically improved in July 1898, by the opening of the eight mile line of the Blackpool & Fleetwood Tramroad Company. Its modern bogie tramcars gave such a reliable service that Blackpool Corporation was shamed into replacing the troublesome conduit system with overhead wires the following year.

In October 1898, the Blackpool, St Annes and Lytham Tramways Company was floated as a public company, issuing 40,000 5 per cent cumulative preference shares and 45,000 £1 ordinary shares to raise a total of £85,000, with plans to replace fixed points by sprung points on the St Annes-Lytham section and to establish a quicker service by providing additional loops, at a cost of £2,500. However a more significant action of the company was to buy out the interests of British Gas Traction, so that it would have a free hand to decide the form of traction to be used on the tramway. In 1900 the depot and gas compressor facilities were moved to the Blackpool side of the boundary at Squires Gate in order to take advantage of the cheaper gas supply offered by Blackpool Corporation.

There were various contemporary schemes for tramways to Preston, and even to Southport across the Ribble estuary, but their only practical result in Lytham was an extension from Market Square along Clifton Street to the Cottage Hospital (East Beach), eventually opened as an electric tramway in September 1903.

Meanwhile there was a shortage of gas trams, so the summer of 1900 saw the mixed operation of gas and horse trams, using 20 old cars purchased from Farnworth. This was unsatisfactory even though bad weather affected traffic, but understandably the company did not want to buy any new gas trams. Trafford Park had none to spare second-hand, but existing cars were speeded up with new gearing pending electrification and the horse cars were stored for emergency use only, being offered for sale in August 1901. On 6th August, 1900,

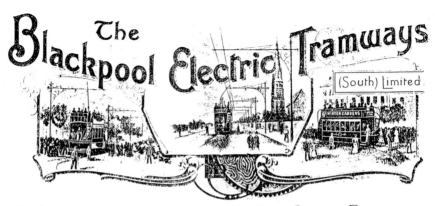

The Blackpool Electric Tramways (South) Limited

AND AT LONDON.

9, CENTRAL BEACH PARADE,

BLACKPOOL.

July, 1901.

Dear Sir,

We forward you under cover, marked 'Private,' a copy of the Prospectus of the above Tramways now being issued to the Public. The issue is made to provide capital for the conversion of existing horse and gas-driven Tramways into Overhead Electric Tramways. Dividends are guaranteed upon the Preference Shares and interest upon the Debenture Stock, during conversion of the line, and commence immediately.

Blackpool is so well known as a holiday resort for people in Lancashire and Yorkshire, and the traffic is so enormous, that very large returns appear to be certain, resulting in substantial Premiums accruing upon the Shares.

The last Blackpool Electric Tramway (Blackpool and Fleetwood) went to an exceptionally high premium, and the Shares are now dealt in at £3 and £4 Premium per Share. The new Company runs in the opposite direction, through a far more populous and increasing district towards the manufacturing town of Preston.

A number of influential Lancashire firms are interested in the scheme, and a large sum has already been privately secured in the district, sufficient to guarantee the success of the issue.

As the matter will only be open for a day or two longer, your application should be sent per return of post to ensure allotment.

Yours faithfully,

THE ELECTRIC TRAMWAYS CONSTRUCTION & MAINTENANCE CO., LTD.,

Contractors.

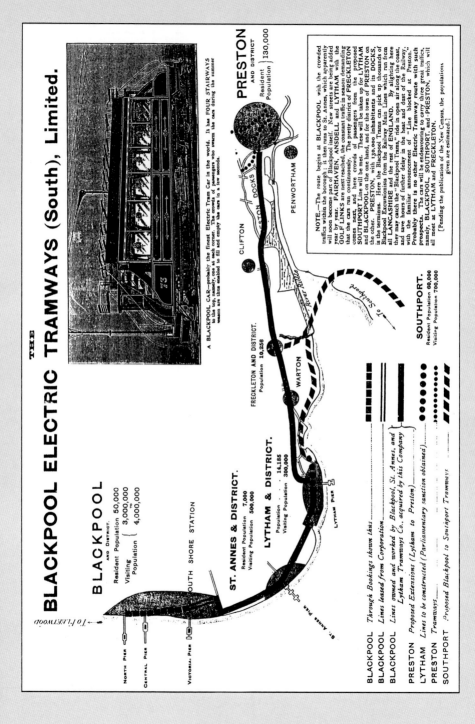

a new Act had authorised the Tramways Company to electrify the tramway, and it was to become double-track except for half a mile through Lytham, but this took some time.

The electric tramway was a symbol of modernity for the new century. Large cities such as Manchester and Glasgow, and smaller towns such as Stockport and Blackpool developed municipally-owned tramway networks as a matter of policy to serve as amenities for the inhabitants. On the other hand less built-up districts were frequently the object of private schemes, which often included the provision of electricity generating plant and the supply of electricity to the area surrounding the tramway. The promotions of steam tramways in the 1880s had included a number of dubious financial transactions, and electric tramways in their turn both offered opportunities to entrepreneurs and gave rise to some schemes which were picturesque speculations at best.

In fact St Annes Urban District Council commenced the supply of electricity to the district on 12th March, 1901, (Lytham had no public electricity supply until after its amalgamation with St Annes in 1922) but the prospects of an electric tramway through the developing areas of South Shore, St Annes and Lytham saw the Blackpool, St Annes and Lytham Tramways Company bought by the Electric Tramways Construction and Maintenance Co. Ltd, in early 1901 for £111,000. The new syndicate talked of extending the tramway from Lytham through Warton to Freckleton (4 miles), where it would run onto a new light railway to Preston , a further 7 miles, quoting annual profits of £21,645 for the Blackpool-Lytham line and £35,866 from the extended line. Their immediate action was to float a public company, Blackpool Electric Tramways (South) Ltd, to buy the tramway from them once it had been electrified, but for legal purposes the Blackpool, St Annes and Lytham Tramways Co. had to continue to operate the line because it had the lease of the line along Lytham Road from Blackpool Corporation and this could not be assigned to any other company.

Permission for the extension was refused (these were the days of a strong railway interest in Parliament which did not take kindly to the idea of new rural light railways running parallel to existing railways), but work on electrification finally began around Squires Gate in December 1902. The most exciting feature of the conversion was the destruction of the gas tram depot at the end of Lytham Road by a gale on 27th February, 1903, wrecking the 13 trams inside, but there were still seven trams available in the small depot on Henry Street in Lytham, and the gas compressor house survived intact, although the gas trams did not run a public service again.

Legally the sections of tramway which were to be electrified within Lytham and St Annes were divided into three. The track which in those days lay within the boundaries of St Annes Urban District Council, from the Blackpool boundary at Squires Gate through the middle of St Annes along Clifton Drive, was Tramway No.1, with a total length of 3 miles 5 furlongs 0.21 chains (3 miles 1105 yards or 5.838 kilometres). Tramway No.2 was the section within the Lytham Urban District from the boundary with St Annes to Clifton Square, a length of 1 mile 7 furlongs 8.46 chains (1 mile 1726 yards or 3.187 kilometres), and the new line to the Cottage Hospital in Lytham became Tramway No.3, with a length expressed as 0 miles 5 furlongs 5.76 chains (1227 yards or 1122 metres).

Chapter Two

The Electric Tramway 1903-1937

By 1903 the construction of a new electric tramway was a relatively routine engineering task, though of course it was still a source of both interest and inconvenience to the inhabitants of the district concerned, and the tramway operator had to ensure that it had a soundly-built tramway which would meet the safety requirements of the Board of Trade. As previously Blackpool Corporation did the work on the section it owned along Lytham Road: the work on the track was estimated to cost £11,600 and the overhead electrical work £6,000 more. The Tramway Company was to pay a 9 per cent annual rental on this outlay for the use of the line, whilst Blackpool Corporation would supply electrical current up to the borough boundary at 2d. per unit for the first 250,000 units and 1.75d. after that, with a minimum guarantee of 150,000 units. St Annes supplied current to the Tramways Company at 2d. per unit for the rest of the line, and the opportunity was taken to light the route with a single 16 candle-power lamp on each pole fitted to a bracket 9 ft from the ground, there were also five 500 candle-power arc lamps in St Annes and six similar lamps in Lytham.

The track was laid on a six inch thick bed of concrete throughout, new rail weighing 90 lb. per yard coming in 60 ft lengths from Walter Scott Ltd, Leeds Steel Works. Points, crossings and other special trackwork in 'Era' patent manganese steel came from Hadfield's Steel Foundry Co. Ltd, Sheffield. (Developed by Sir Robert Hadfield manganese steel was particularly popular for tramway crossings because approximately 13 per cent manganese gave it the property of work-hardening, actually getting harder with the impact of tramcar wheels.) The overhead wires were suspended from bracket arms extending from steel poles at the side of the road: whilst it was obvious that the poles rose 24 feet into the air it was also important that they were sunk 6 feet into the ground. The hundreds of poles required were supplied by Walter Macfarlane & Co. of Glasgow.

The most spectacular event during the conversion of the tramway was the collapse of the main gas tram depot , but fortunately the workmen who had been due to gather there at that time before going out on the electrification work had been delayed by the bad weather and there were no human casualties. Unfortunately an accident near St Cuthbert's Church a fortnight previously, on 12th February, had sadder consequences. A gas tram was pulling a bogie wagon loaded with six steel traction poles for the overhead wires when Mr John Boardman, a labourer living at Hawes Side in Marton, tried to board it: tragically he slipped and was run over by the loaded wagon, being killed instantly.

Though the extension to Lytham Hospital was delayed until September by men being transferred to tramway projects in other towns, the first 10 trams arrived in May 1903, and the current was switched on during Wednesday night, 20th May, and the first trial run was made the following morning from Squires

During the conversion to electric operation the track gang take the opportunity to be photographed on one of the larger gas trams and a four-wheel trailer amongst the sandhills.
TD Collection

No.5 has attracted a crowd of onlookers on its first trial run into Lytham from the depot at Squires Gate on 21st May, 1903. The bicycle appears to have an acetylene headlamp.
TD Collection

Gate to Fairhaven. On 27th May Mr Alexander P. Trotter inspected the electrical equipment of the line for the Board of Trade, then on Thursday 28th May Major Druitt inspected and accepted the route, stipulating speed limits of 12 mph along Lytham Road, 4 mph round Squires Gate corner, 14 mph along Clifton Drive, 4 mph round Ansdell corner, 10 mph along Ansdell Road, Cambridge Road and Church Road, and 8 mph in Market Square, Lytham. The report of the inspection in the *Lytham Times* recorded: 'The car travelled along Clifton Drive at 18 miles an hour, and could have done 20.' The 10 trams were available for the first public service on Saturday 30th May, with another 20 on order for the summer season, supplied by the British Thomson-Houston Company of Rugby but actually constructed by the British Electric Car Company, a short-lived firm of the 1900s tramway boom whose trams gained a reputation for poor construction.

The first Sunday morning of operation, 31st May, saw an accident occur near Fairhaven Hotel. A visitor, Mr Baxendale, was travelling on the open top deck of a tram as it passed the horse-drawn tower wagon used for gaining access to the overhead wires. As the tram passed the horse took fright and overturned the tower wagon, causing the platform to fall heavily onto the tram and knock Mr Baxendale unconscious with a 2-inch long wound to his head.

For the winter of 1903 the Tramways Company reduced fares: 4*d*. from Clifton Square, Lytham, all the way to South Shore terminus, 2*d*. to St Annes (2*d*. from St Annes to South Shore), and halfpenny fares on the new line to the Cottage Hospital, mentioned as being useful for Shipyard employees in those days.

1904 was a year of crisis for the Tramways Company, despite the fact that it carried plenty of passengers and employed 120 men in the summer and 60 in the winter, with another 6 men working permanently on the track. The root of the problem was that the funds raised by the issue of shares had been insufficient to cover both the purchase of the gas tramway and the subsequent conversion to electric traction. The shortfall was made good by issuing £150,000 debentures paying a fixed interest to the holders, but when the funds of the company proved inadequate to pay this interest the debenture holders held a crisis meeting in December 1904. Even by the standards of the turn of the century the new tramway had gone bust pretty quickly!

There now arose a slightly Gilbertian situation in which the growing districts of Lytham and St Annes combined Edwardian gentility with a public transport service worked by the trustees of the debenture holders, the original shareholders having very little hope of financial recompense.

A major problem more easily overcome was the refusal of Blackpool Corporation to allow Lytham trams closer to the centre of Blackpool than South Shore. Such obstruction was not acceptable to Edwardian legislators, and a impasse of this kind in Newcastle-on-Tyne was resolved by Parliament granting the company involved compulsory running powers over Newcastle Corporation tracks into the city centre. With its position strengthened by this precedent the Tramways Company threatened to apply for similar compulsory running powers through to Talbot Square in Blackpool. Blackpool Corporation now realised that they would have to grant some sort of access, but carefully

With the public service established, a bracket arm supporting the overhead wires frames No.2 as its runs along Clifton Drive South towards St Annes Square (near St Thomas Road). The photographer has caught the conductor's eye. *T. Morris Collection*

This view of No.12 emphasizes that in the years before World War I the roads between South Shore and St Annes were not the wide avenues they are now. *JG Collection*

arranged the routes so as to minimise any loss of revenue from its own Promenade services. Accordingly, once the relevant tracks were physically connected at South Shore in July 1905, through cars from Lytham ran to Central station in Blackpool by turning right at the Royal Oak into Waterloo Road, then following Central Drive to reach a terminus at its junction with Bank Hey Street and Adelaide Street on the inland side of Central station. Lytham cars were also allowed to run the quarter-mile down Station Road to reach the Promenade opposite South Pier (then Victoria Pier), and to run along the rest of Lytham Road to the Manchester Hotel, without being permitted onto the Promenade tracks.

The payment details agreed in 1905 are of interest. Down Station Road to South Pier was a flat £250 per annum, whilst along the rest of Lytham Road to Manchester Square Blackpool Corporation took 1*d*. for each through passenger in either direction as well as all the short distance fares over the section, but this was offset by the Corporation paying the company 2*d*. for each car mile operated north of South Shore station. The arrangements for the cars through to Central station were the same as those for the Manchester Square cars, with a stipulation that the company was to operate a 15-minute service in winter and a car every 7½ minutes in summer. For all three routes Blackpool Corporation supplied traction current but the Lytham cars kept their own drivers and conductors. The agreement also gave Blackpool Corporation running powers for its trams through to Lytham, but these were used very rarely for special occasions such as the 1909 Air Display at Squires Gate. There was quite enough traffic for Blackpool trams within their existing bounds and the Lytham trams came to provide useful additional capacity, especially since the Tramways Company bought a batch of 10 double-deck open-top crossbench cars from the Brush Electrical Engineering Company at Loughborough for the summer traffic to and from Blackpool, and a trip to St Annes or Lytham became a significant attraction for visitors.

From South Shore station or Victoria Pier to St Annes was 4*d*., to Lytham 6*d*., whilst the extra fare from Central station was merely the 1*d*. payable to Blackpool Corporation, but the extra traffic promised much for the future, 17,758 passengers being carried over these three routes in the first four days of operation. The open-sided cars were particularly popular - our Edwardian forefathers wore plenty of clothing even on holiday - so over the winter 10 of the original cars were sent to the United Electric Car Company at Preston (successors to the British Electric Car Company) for conversion to a similar condition, returning to traffic in the summer of 1906. The remaining 20 saloon cars were considered sufficient for winter services.

The annual general meeting at the end of 1905 reflected the troubled finances of the tramway. Despite the through-running agreement with Blackpool receipts had only increased to £20,957 from £20,357 the previous year, and since the tramway had not taken the minimum agreed amount of electricity from Blackpool Corporation there was a useless £310 to be paid on that account, the total electricity bill being £4,209 16*s*. 6*d*. In addition there was an item for 200 guineas (£210) for fees to the trustees of the debenture holders. It was claimed that the electricity charges of 2*d*. per unit were very high, a figure of 0.25*d*. per

Map of Through Running by Lytham St Annes Trams over Blackpool Corporation Tracks July 1905-January 1923

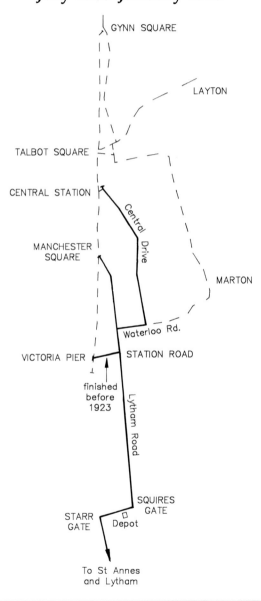

unit elsewhere being quoted. The lower figure seems optimistic - low figures for tramways which generated their own current quoted in 1904 were 0.38*d*. in Newcastle upon Tyne and 0.39*d*. in Huddersfield (including maintenance but nothing for the capital cost of the generating plant) - but agreements made around that time between Bootle Corporation and the Liverpool Corporation Tramways, and between Grimsby Corporation and the Great Grimsby Street Tramways Company both involved a maximum charge of 1.5*d*. per unit compared with the 2*d*. payable by the Lytham tramways.

With the new agreement concluded with Blackpool there was now no need for both the companies previously established to remain in existence; accordingly a scheme was devised to wind up Blackpool Electric Tramways (South) and distribute the shares which it held in the old company (the Blackpool, St Annes and Lytham Tramways Co.) among its shareholders, each preference shareholder to receive a proportionate number of the 50,000 5 per cent Cumulative Preference Shares of 18*s*. fully paid (totalling £45,000), and every ordinary shareholder to receive a proportionate number of the 100,000 16*s*. fully paid Ordinary Shares (totalling £80,000).

The tramway settled down to the years which would subsequently be looked back upon as a pre-war golden age, and for those of the Lancashire population who were able to visit the Fylde Coast for holidays a ride on the top deck through to Lytham or St Annes on a fine day must have seemed confirmation that the Victorian desire for progress was indeed being realised. There was continuing and significant development in amenities which would attract visitors to the towns: whilst Lytham developed Lowther Gardens primarily for local residents, St Annes Pier had been doubled in width in 1903, in 1910 it gained the Floral Hall, seating over 800, and the following year the rival Cosy Corner Pavilion opened with accommodation for no less than 1,700 people. Even Princess Louise joined the throng in 1912, opening Princess Parade in Blackpool, then being driven by Mr George Wood, the traffic manager, down Clifton Drive to Lytham and back.

Meanwhile the finances of the tramway settled down to their own surreal stability. At the end of 1906 the balance of profit was £6,899, £1,500 was transferred to the sinking fund and 2½ per cent was paid on account of the balance due on the debentures. The summer of 1907 was regarded as wet, but there were still traffic receipts of £27,490, of which £4,745 was payable to Blackpool Corporation. Other significant outgoings were:

Traffic expenses	£4,005
General expenses	£3,010
General repairs & maintenance	£2,384
Power expenses	£5,292
Rents of leased lines & bank interest	£2,359

Total expenditure of £17,051 1*s*. 7*d*. left a balance of profit of £6,500 5*s*. 1½*d*., but unfortunately the debenture interest falling due was £7,500, so again 2½ per cent was paid on account and £1,500 was transferred to the sinking fund.

However in subsequent years the figure for traffic receipts was more typically between £24,000 and £25,000; for example 1912 produced receipts of £24,438 from a total car mileage of 700,592 (approximately 8.4*d*. per mile). Despite 1912 being a wet year the company still declared that it could not afford to fit covered tops to the trams. But, fortunately, good weather in 1913 brought a significant increase in traffic: receipts of £28,389 being generated by a car mileage of 761,779 (average revenue also increasing to approximately 8.9*d*. per mile). Nevertheless the balance for the year was still only £5,066, and the tramway continued to be run by the trustees of the debenture holders.

But operationally the tramway can be regarded as a success. A late-duty cashier arriving at Squires Gate Depot in mid-afternoon could see that he was going to have a busy evening if he looked inside the sheds and found them empty: all 40 trams were out in traffic. In 1913 the Tramways and Light Railways Association held its 5th Annual Conference at Blackpool: its souvenir brochure recorded the total number of passengers carried annually by the Company as approximately 3,750,000, whilst the population of St Annes had grown from about 2,000 at the time the cars started running from Blackpool to a resident population of between 11,000 and 12,000, and a visiting population of 30,000 in the summer months. Children's camps and convalescent homes had come to rub shoulders with golf courses, the Marine Lake at Fairhaven, St Annes Promenade and many other amenities. The writer particularly mentions the new Clifton Park Racecourse, built on the site of the Aviation Ground at Squires Gate, he little guessed the changes which two world wars were going to bring to this area.

Traffic manager Mr George Wood wrote a fascinating series of articles under the heading 'Hints To Motormen' in the monthly employees' magazine between March and October 1914, including the following notes on traffic receipts quoted verbatim:

Traffic Receipts

We give below our Traffic Receipts for five weeks ending July 2nd 1914, also receipts for the corresponding five weeks of last year:-

Last Year				*This Year*			
	£	s.	d.		£	s.	d.
June 5th	501	0	1½	June 4th	957	18	4
June 12th	427	19	9	June 11th	684	2	8
June 19th	539	12	1	June 18th	561	8	1½
June 26th	551	4	9	June 25th	531	19	2
July 3rd	808	12	5	July 2nd	813	0	8
Totals	£2828	9	1½		£3548	8	11½

An increase of £719.19.10 over the corresponding five weeks of last year. The aggregate to date being £12,113 as against £12,156 for the previous year.

Mr Wood describes the route in meticulous detail from the point of view of a motorman instructing a learner, right from taking the tram out of the depot in the morning:

. . . some of our drivers might think that I am wrong here and that it is the brasswork which should be cleaned first - but that is a mistake because when examining the car you might find a fault with it which could not be remedied before you were due out and this would necessitate your cleaning another car. Whilst examining your car do not forget the lifeguards, sand hoppers, sand pipes, sand punch, door catches, point bars, drawbars and see that each circuit of lights is right and that the spare lamp is good, and under no circumstances, tell your learner, he must never [sic] bring a car out of Depot without first trying the electric brake.

Mr Wood mentions the route up to the Manchester Hotel as being run 'in the season' but omits the short section down Station Road to South Pier - this had not been operated since 1912. The various schools along the route, awkward stretches of wiring, the level crossing at St Paul's Avenue used by the Fairhaven Estate engine travelling to and from Ansdell Station sidings, the importance of not getting the tram stuck on blown sand and thus losing electrical contact with the rails by going too far up the loop at the Cottage Hospital terminus, all receive due attention in Mr Wood's notes.

World War I was in many ways a time of financial prosperity for the Fylde Coast, though monetary figures quoted must be viewed in the light of the great wartime increase in prices. The circumstances of the time meant that at the end of 1916 the company could report that all its 'conductors' were women, and that it had had a record year. Traffic receipts had increased to £46,893, of which £10,123 was payable to Blackpool (this proportion had increased slightly to 21.6 per cent from the 17.3 per cent of 1907). The figures for major outgoings were:

Traffic expenses	£7,848
General expenses	£3,742
General repairs & maintenance	£7,535
Power expenses	£5,046
Rent of leased lines	£2,294

Overall there was a profit balance of £11,714 in these wartime conditions.

Along the coast Blackpool was also gaining: training camps brought troops to the town all the year round instead of the seasonal influx of visitors, the Corporation used tramway facilities for the manufacture of shells, and there grew a feeling that too many of the local attractions lay outside the Borough boundaries, and hence outside the control of the Corporation. As far as the tramways in the area were concerned, the first change came on 26th July, 1917, when the 21-year lease of the original section of line used by the gas trams on Lytham Road expired and was not renewed, a serious blow to the Tramways Company since from that date all receipts on Lytham Road were paid to Blackpool Corporation, Blackpool trams commenced a service to Squires Gate, and a request to run Lytham trams direct to Central station via Manchester Square and the Promenade was refused.

At this time Blackpool Corporation was taking over the Blackpool & Fleetwood Tramroad, Alderman Lindsay Parkinson making the arrangements personally in 1918 until the take-over could be formally authorised by an Act of Parliament the following year. The Council next intended to buy the Blackpool,

Top Left: Mr H.W. Laing, General Manager *JG Collection*

Above: Mr Laing on the right, Mr Woods (traffic manager) on the left, outside the Lytham Road offices.

JG Collection

Left: As Mayor of Lytham St Annes, Alderman C.F. Critchley proudly poses at the controls of the Corporation's first new tram, No.41.　　*IM Collection*

St Annes and Lytham Tramways Company, actually approving plans for a large central car works for the Greater Blackpool Tramways in November, 1918.
It was too late. Lytham had little desire for Blackpool-style mass tourism, whilst St Annes had developed a policy of catering on a smaller scale than Blackpool for a more discerning type of visitor. The St Annes on the Sea Improvement Act of 1914 authorised the tasteful extension of the South Promenade at a cost of £2,600, the same year Lord Ashton financed the purchase and improvement of what became the Ashton Gardens (to the extent of a most generous £26,000), then in 1916 a large open-air pool the size of sixteen typical swimming baths gave St Annes an attraction for thousands. Neither town was going to become a satellite of Blackpool.

A traffic boom in 1919 meant that the Lytham tramways could carry over 80,000 passengers on a good summer's day, but wartime inflation had roughly trebled costs such as wages (by this time traffic staff varied from 80 in the winter to 200 in the summer) and there was a serious backlog of repairs to the track and the cars to be made good. Nevertheless the local authorities did not want to hand the management of such an important service to Blackpool Corporation. In 1921 the lease on the Lytham and St Annes section would expire, and St Annes UDC had first option, much to the annoyance of Blackpool, and the opposition of the Lancashire & Yorkshire Railway Company. Lytham UDC also considered acquiring that part of the tramway which lay within its boundaries, but a Bill to permit such a purchase was rejected by the Standing Orders Committee of the House of Lords, and they agreed that St Annes UDC should buy the Tramways Company outright. St Annes made an offer for the company which was accepted in November, 1919, and the purchase was completed on 28th October, 1920, a total of £144,936 being paid. The transaction was financed by a loan of £132,279 4s. 8d., repayable over 30 years.

Despite the fact that the total capital expenditure of the Tramways Company had amounted to £284,500, this was an enormous sum of money at the time for St Annes to pay (the recent open-air pool had cost £10,000 for example), and it was necessary to justify the price paid. Councillors explained that they were wary of what sum might be awarded to the company by compulsory arbitration if they were taken over at the end of the lease in 1921. It was said that the local authority not very far away in Colne had ended up paying 50 per cent more than their tramway company had actually asked for, and with this in mind it seemed sensible to agree a price which reflected the happy relations between the council and the company.

It should perhaps be mentioned at this stage that 1920 buses were unreliable, cost twice as much to run as trams, and were very much looked down upon - certainly not an appropriate means of transport for the status-conscious inhabitants of Lytham and St Annes (or even for their servants?).

Council ownership was soon shown by the inscription 'St Annes Council Tramways' on the upper deck panels (traditionally known as decency panels for obscuring any possible views of ladies' ankles), the blue and cream company livery changed slightly to blue and ivory, and perhaps most obvious was the removal of almost all the many external advertisements including those on the seat backs and the stairs, leaving only a neat poster board at each end of the upper decks to satisfy the terms of an ongoing contract for advertising various attractions owned by the Blackpool Tower Co.

The year 1921 saw the tramways enter the petrol age with the acquisition of a Halley motor tower wagon and a Ford van for carrying rail groove deepening and grinding equipment. The General Manager subsequently reported that weather which was too wet for welding work (such as building up crossings) was ideal for rail grinding. Adversely the coal strike of 1921 saw tramway operation suspended for three Sundays in June.

Further possible expansion by Blackpool was thwarted in 1922 when St Annes and Lytham merged to form the Borough of Lytham St Annes, bringing another change of title to Lytham St Annes Corporation Tramways, then Blackpool Corporation finally agreed to permit Lytham trams to run up the Promenade to Talbot Square from the Manchester Hotel. This started on 22nd January, 1923, prompted by the track on Central Drive being relaid. The Lytham St Annes Corporation Act of 1923 gave the new borough powers to operate buses as well as trams, the first bus services starting the same year, but the tramway was still very much the first priority and the following year a batch of 10 new top-covered trams (Nos.41-50) came from English Electric at Preston. The General Manager, Mr Laing, had specified trams of a high standard of comfort and they came to be known as Pullman cars - it was even claimed that there was enough headroom on both decks for a man to stand up wearing a top hat. The depot at Squires Gate was specially extended to accommodate these trams.

Services in the borough were maintained during the General Strike in 1926 by the expedient of turning out office staff on the trams, but on 23rd July of that year a decision taken the previous January was implemented and the extension out to the Cottage Hospital was taken out of use (although it remained intact until after it had been formally abandoned in October 1928). A bus service to Meadow Lane replaced the trams. However the same day (23rd July, 1926) saw Lytham trams reach as far north as Gynn Square in Blackpool, primarily to reduce the congestion being caused by trams reversing at Talbot Square but also giving useful connections to the north side of Blackpool. In later years Blackpool Corporation hired the 20 crossbench cars for the period of the Illuminations in the autumn, and in these circumstances Lytham trams actually ran all the way up past the Cabin to Bispham.

Blackpool Corporation extended the Promenade tramway from the Pleasure Beach down the new South Promenade to Starr Gate in 1926, but at that time no connection was made with the Lytham tracks. In the following year three of the original 1903 cars were refurbished, and the General Manager reported himself happy with the condition of both the trams and the track.

In July 1928, the Lytham tramways entered what was to prove to be their final phase when a connection was made between the Blackpool and Lytham tracks at Starr Gate. From this time two basic 15-minute services were operated between Lytham and Gynn Square, one via Lytham Road and the other via South Promenade. The crossbench cars worked holiday extras as required to Talbot Square or Central station from Fairhaven or St Annes, the fare between St Annes and Central station now being 7d.

The problems of drifting sand along the dunes between Starr Gate and St Annes have been put down to the trampling of the starr grass by the crowds at the old aviation meetings, or alternatively to the training of troops during World War I. In any event by December 1929, the situation had become so serious that on two days westerly gales actually blocked the tram tracks with sand and a bus service had to be substituted. However tram 26 had been converted into a single-deck works car, fitted with sweeping brushes, grinding and welding equipment; its most important duty was keeping the tracks clear of sand, and in 1931 sandscreens were installed along Clifton Drive North.

Meanwhile the relative prosperity of the 1920s had been overtaken by the American Wall Street Crash of 1929. Towards the end of the decade the tramways had been making a gross annual profit of around £8,000, swallowed up by loan charges of around £11,000 to produce a small annual deficit of about £3,000. (In purely financial terms it could be said that the Council had actually paid too much for the Tramways Company since the earning power of the tramway had proved to be insufficient to pay the loan charges on the money borrowed to pay for the deal.) However the financial year 1929-30 saw the gross profit dip to £4,605, which the loan charges took to an overall loss more than doubled to £6,712. Nor were the infant bus services any better: loan charges against them meant that they showed an overall loss of £2,550 the same year, though it is interesting that the average fare paid on the feeder bus routes was 1.69d. compared with 2.72d. on the long tram route (where the many through Blackpool passengers brought up the average).

Then came the national financial crisis of 1931 and it was said that the total expenditure on the trams over the previous ten years had been £175,821, but that this had merely resulted in a cumulative loss of £50,000. Private talks were even held with the London Midland and Scottish Railway (successors to the Lancashire & Yorkshire Railway) about a possible sale of the trams and buses. But current supplied to the tramways was worth £1,000 each year to the borough electricity department, and the trams were still important for bringing visitors to the town even though traffic had dropped to the point that 32 cars were sufficient to cater for the summer peak. A decision was taken in 1932 to keep the trams in the face of the repeated annual losses. Much of the fleet was reaching 30 years in traffic, but the opportunity arose to acquire trams second-hand from operators which were closing their tramways, four small single-deckers from the Dearne District Light Railways (Nos.51-54) and a large bogie double-decker from Accrington Corporation (No.55 - 'Big Bertha') arriving in 1933, then a four-wheel double-decker from Preston Corporation (No.56) the year after.

The financial position of the tramway in the mid-1930s is summarised in the following table, in each case the figures refer to the financial year ending 31st March of the year mentioned, but naturally the heaviest traffic would be carried in the summer of the previous year.

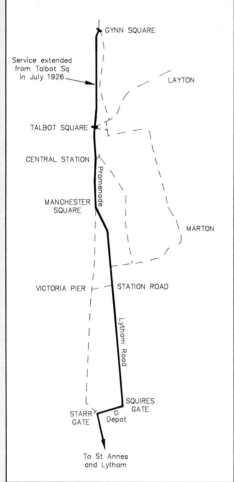

Map of Through Running by Lytham St Annes Trams over Blackpool Corporation Transport Tracks January 1923-July 1928

GYNN SQUARE

Service extended from Talbot Sq in July 1926

LAYTON

TALBOT SQUARE

CENTRAL STATION

Promenade

MANCHESTER SQUARE

MARTON

VICTORIA PIER

STATION ROAD

Lytham Road

SQUIRES GATE

STARR GATE

Depot

To St Annes and Lytham

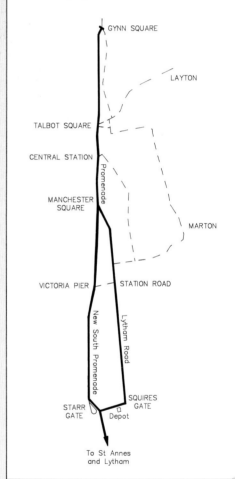

Map of Through Running by Lytham St Annes Trams over Blackpool Corporation Transport Tracks July 1928-March 1937

GYNN SQUARE

LAYTON

TALBOT SQUARE

CENTRAL STATION

Promenade

MANCHESTER SQUARE

MARTON

VICTORIA PIER

STATION ROAD

New South Promenade

Lytham Road

STARR GATE

SQUIRES GATE

Depot

To St Annes and Lytham

| | 1934 | 1935 | 1936 |
	£	£	£
Traffic Revenue	27,379	25,205	23,381
Through Running Expenses)	14,178	14,704	13,772
from Blackpool + sundries)			
Total Revenue	41,478	40,089	37,425
Gross Profit	6,040	6,186	5,508
Interest on Mortgage	5,243	4,865	4,185
Sinking Fund Contributions	5,435	5,627	5,749
Net Loss	4,858	5,524	4,697
Omnibus Net Profit	1,632	865	2,864

A few details from the year ending 31st March, 1935:

| Highest weekly traffic receipts | £1106 13s. 10d. | (w/e 14th August) |
| Lowest weekly traffic receipts | £219 8s. 0d. | (w/e 15th January) |

| Passengers carried including through running | 6,729,103 |
| Passengers carried on own lines | 3,397,050 |

In view of the Edwardian controversy about paying 2d. per unit for electricity it is interesting to see that the contemporary price had come down to 0.63d. per unit, comparing well with the national average quoted at 0.865d. per unit.

However the most important figure for many people was the budgeted loss of £5,000 for the financial year 1935-36, equivalent to a 4d. rate. In contrast the buses had moved into a position where they were making a net profit. It is often stated that the better economics of bus operation in the 1930s derived from the lower fuel consumption of diesel buses taking over from the previous petrol buses, but this is not the case here since Lytham St Annes only started running its first three diesel buses in September 1935, and it would appear that the improvement was a result of judicious operating economies.

The end of the tramways was to come fairly quickly. In 1935 a proposal to fit windscreens to all the trams was rejected, and on 7th June a new express bus service from Lytham through to Blackpool was inaugurated. At this time Blackpool was carrying out a great modernisation of its tramways and in September 1935 Blackpool Corporation offered to buy the Lytham St Annes undertaking, offering £116,000 to wipe out the accumulated debt together with relaying through to St Annes (which would have been an extension of the Promenade reserved track) and new trams. It is said that the slightly wider wheels of Blackpool trams would have caught the granite setts of the roadway on either side of the existing Lytham St Annes rails; in any case the new Blackpool trams were so much wider, and longer even than Big Bertha, that it would almost certainly have been necessary to realign the tracks in places to given the appropriate clearances between two trams passing, especially on curves. A foretaste of what was on offer had occurred on 13th October, 1933,

LYTHAM TRAMS

In contrast to the bracket arms seen previously in St Annes, the Lytham Road track built by Blackpool Corporation had the overhead wiring supported by span-wires strung between pairs of traction poles. No.16 is showing the destination 'Victoria Pier' (now the South Pier at Blackpool).
IM Collection

when the prototype Blackpool railcoach (No.200) had taken a party of Yorkshire transport managers non-stop from St Annes to Fleetwood and then brought them back to St Annes in 45 minutes, presumably late at night after the normal tram services had finished.

This would have been a logical way of securing the future of the tramway, but by now there was a significant feeling in the borough that the future lay in developing the residential side of the district rather than being dependent on large numbers of holidaymakers brought down by tram from Blackpool. In particular people looked across to Southport, which had withdrawn its trams at the end of 1934, then in December 1935 neighbouring Preston also lost its trams. Accordingly the proposed sale to Blackpool was defeated in Lytham St Annes Council, and it was decided to borrow £18,330 to buy new diesel buses to replace the trams.

Permission to operate the replacement bus services was granted by the Traffic Commissioners on 5th December, 1936, and they took over from the trams between Lytham and St Annes on 15th December. Delivery of the rest of the replacement buses enabled the remaining tramway services to close on 27th March except for the cars from St Annes to Gynn Square via the Promenade. The final section between Squires Gate and St Annes Square closed after a ceremonial last journey by No.41 on 28th April, 1937, driven from St Annes Square to Squires Gate Depot by the Mayor of Lytham St Annes, Councillor C.H.Riley J.P., with fares collected by Councillor J.W. Horsfall, who had been largely responsible for defeating the take-over by Blackpool. After the optimism of its early years the life of the tramway had been relatively short, and one of the passengers on the last tram, Mr J. Bowman, formerly Editor of the *Lytham St Annes Express*, had also ridden on the first gas tram, the first electric tram and the first tram under municipal ownership.

The track and overhead wires vanished except for the connection along Squires Gate Lane past the depot, which linked the Blackpool Corporation tracks at Starr Gate with the Lytham Road line. This continued to be used by Blackpool Circular Tours up to 1939, but it still remained intact and from 1957 it was used again for tours until the Lytham Road tramway closed in October 1961.

The tramways had served Lytham and St Annes well, but it is paradoxical that if the defeated Blackpool take-over had taken place the section to St Annes Square at least would have almost certainly have lasted until the Blackpool closures of the early 1960s, and might even have been running to this day.

The track gang demonstrates the important work of keeping the rails clear of sand (No.43 stands behind). *West Lancs. Evening Gazette*

No.41 became the last tram after only 13 years in traffic. From left to right on the front of the tram are: Councillor J.W. Horsfall, Councillor C.H. Riley. Mr J.C. Fairchild (Electricity and Transport Manager). *Evening Gazette*

Chapter Three

Rolling Stock

Gas Trams 1-4

Built 1896, Ashbury Railway Carriage & Iron Co., Manchester
40 seats (24 up, 16 down)   Weight 7½-8 tons   Cost £700 each
Water-cooled 15hp horizontally-opposed twin-cylinder Otto gas engine built by Gas
Motorenfabrik Deutz of Cologne in Germany

The engine was fitted under the seats on one side of the lower deck, with a
flywheel housed between the engine and the outside panelling of the tram, the
panelling incorporating hinged opening panels for access. The town gas (coal
gas) fuel was stored at a pressure of 120psi (8 bar) in three cylinders, one under
the downstairs seats opposite the engine and the other two slung transversely
under the car at each end. A spark from a battery ignited the gas charge in the
cylinders on each stroke, and it was possible to run the engine on one cylinder
when it was idling or only running on light load, the running speeds of the
engine being 80rpm and 260rpm.

Each driving platform had a moveable lever, which was in the upright
position with the tram stationary and the engine idling. To start the tram this
lever was pushed to the left, putting the tram into gear via a friction clutch, then
the lever could be pushed to the right and a full supply of gas brought into
action another clutch with higher gearing to give the car its maximum speed. A
second lever worked the crawler gear, which could also be used as a brake. The
speed on the level was only about that of a horse tram (6-9mph), and when
going uphill progress slowed to 2-3mph. There was a disagreeable smell of gas
about the cars, and the rough riding was not helped by all the seats being
wooden: a longitudinal seat for eight passengers running the length of each
side of the saloon downstairs, then eight reversible double garden seats split
either side of a centre aisle and a bench seat for four passengers at each end on
top. Contemporary reports suggest that the engines were rougher when idling
at 80rpm on one cylinder, then better when running along unless the crawler
gear was engaged.

The rocker panels on the lower deck and the dashes were royal blue with gold
lining, whilst the rest of the bodywork was cream with royal blue lining.

Two cars were available for the opening of the line between South Shore and
St Annes on 11th July, 1896, and the other two entered service later in the year
(including No.4, which had been running in Paris between Landy gas works
and Saint Ouen Gate to demonstrate gas traction). In 1900 the gearing on these
four small trams was altered to enable them to run faster.

After the gas trams stopped running in 1903 some of the ones which were not
destroyed when the depot collapsed were sold to the Provincial Gas Traction
Co. for their 4-mile tramway through Neath in South Wales.

The gas trams survived in Neath until 1920, but one of the small cars was

One of the small gas trams takes on a full load. *JG Collection*

Basically a self-propelled horse car, No.1 shows how the Tramways Company title had to be squeezed onto the short body, as it stands outside Stony Hill Depot in 1896. *IM Collection*

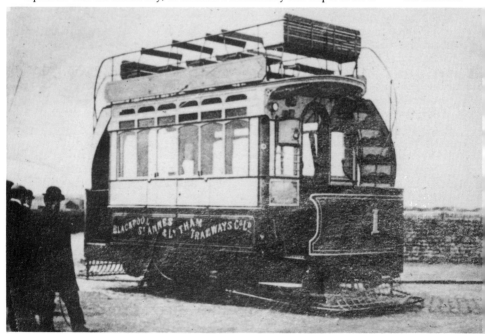

Two of the gas cylinders are visible under either end of the body of No.1. *TD Collection*

No.15 and a landau at the Lytham terminus in 1897. *Jim Ingham Collection*

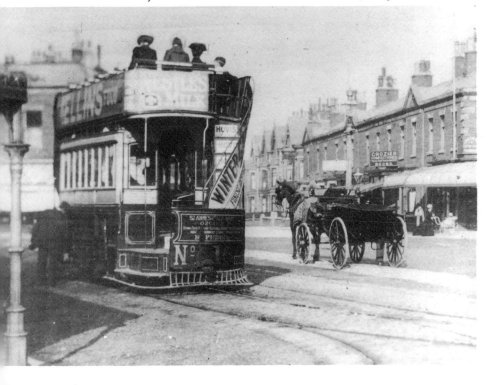

Passengers pose for the photographer of No.16 in 1899. *JG Collection*

No.17 in action near Seafield Road in Lytham. Some of the passengers on the top deck appear to be holding on to their hats. *TD Collection*

Nos.17 and 14 meet at a passing loop near St Annes Congregational Church.

Pete Carr Collection

rescued from a garden in Melyn in 1984 and has been restored (though without an engine) by the Neath Borough Council Training Agency. The identity of this particular car is not known, and it is now thought that the livery of the cars was chocolate and cream rather than the green and ivory which it carries, but its restoration is a credit to Neath and it would be appropriate if it could return to the Fylde in 1996 on the occasion of the centenary of the Lytham St Annes tramways.

Gas trams 5-20

Built 1897, Lancaster Carriage and Wagon Co., Lancaster
52 seats (30 up, 22 down)

These were a larger version of the small trams, acquired for the extension of the tramway from St Annes to Lytham. They had the same motors and controllers as the small cars but better gearing gave them a top speed of 12mph.
Some cars had their stairs panelled, including Nos.8, 12, 14, 15, 17. After the end of the gas trams in 1903 some of these larger cars went to Neath with the small cars, but one saloon body survived on the South Shore sand dunes near the Star Inn as a hut for gypsy fortune-tellers until they left in 1910.

Horse trams

Because of mechanical trouble with the gas trams, 22 horse cars were bought for the 1900 season from Farnworth Urban District Council, near Bolton, bringing the tram fleet to 40.
Seventeen of these were double-deck Eades patent reversible cars, on which the whole body swung round to face the opposite direction at the terminus (saving the weight of the steps at one end), whilst the other three were steam tram trailers formerly used as workmen's cars by the Blackburn & Over Darwen Tramways Co.
The horses were stabled on the site of the present Squires Gate Depot, but to date no photos have been found of the horse cars in service on the tramway.
In December 1900, it was stated in the annual report of the tramways company that 'the horse tram fleet had been given a full and fair trial but the running of them however did not come up to expectations and it is not intended to run them again except in cases of emergency', the cars all being offered for sale in August 1901.

Electric Tram Fleet Introduction

By 1903 the electric tram was becoming an established mode of transport with known characteristics. Unfortunately it has to be said that the Electric Tramways Construction & Maintenance Co. seemed more interested in the profitability of the Blackpool & Fleetwood Tramroad than in observing and emulating certain basic principles which would be obvious to the least technically-minded tram enthusiast of a later generation. The Blackpool &

The gypsy's grounded tram body shows the complicated monitor roof, which gave ventilation to the lower saloon. *IM Collection*

A brand new Lytham tram (possibly No.1) on the traverser at the British Electric Car Co. works in Trafford Park, Manchester. *IM Collection*

Fleetwood cars were fast bogie single-deckers capable of exceeding 20mph and, apart from short town sections at each end, their line was on its own reserved track away from other road-users for its journey of just over 8 miles. In contrast the line through St Annes and Lytham, nearly as long, and again an interurban line running from town to town with little intermediate traffic in the early days, stuck to the existing roads and (partly because of this) was equipped with short-wheelbase four-wheel double-deckers of the same type as were used for the densest urban routes in Liverpool. A design less suited to interurban running it would be hard to imagine, and it is perhaps just as well that the line was not continued from Lytham through to Preston with such cars.

Through running right into Blackpool in 1905 prompted the purchase of a batch of 10 seasonal cars from Brush. The Brush works had supplied the crossbench open-toppers of the Douglas Head Marine Drive tramway in the previous decade and it now provided a modernised version of these on 9ft wheelbase trucks, 10 of the earlier Lytham cars being reconstructed to match them the following winter (though these retained their original 6ft wheelbase trucks).

For the basic service and winter running the tramway relied on the original open-toppers in 1903 condition, until municipalisation brought the 10 Pullman cars from English Electric in 1924, mounted on long wheelbase trucks. The early 1930s saw the purchase of three different types of tram in the second-hand market, including the only bogie car to run in Lytham service, but none of them proved entirely satisfactory. If the tramways had continued after 1937 there would have been the choice of picking up the best cars from other tramways which were closing (as Sunderland did) or buying a batch of new cars, but this was not to be.

No.3 at Lytham Square on Saturday 6th August, 1933. Note the lack of 'Lytham St. Annes' lettering on the tram side.   R. Elliott

No.4 leaving Gynn Square terminus in 1935 in the 'zig-zag' livery of bright blue and brilliant white, first seen on No.15 in 1932.   *IM Collection*

No.6 as refurbished with a 21E truck in 1927, on the depot fan at Squires Gate. Note the beautifully-kept gardens behind, a very attractive part of this small system.

Official photograph

Electric Tram Fleet Summary

	1-30	31-40	21-30	41-50	51-54	55	56
Built (Rebuilt)	1903	1905	(1906)	1924	1924	1915	(1928/29)
Builder	BEC	Brush	UEC	EE	EE	Brush	Preston Corp
Type	DD/OT	DD/CB	DD/CB	DD/OB	SD/TE	DD/TE	DD/TE
Length o/a	27'6"	29'9"	27'6"	31'0"	32'0"	35'0"	28'6"
Width o/a	7'0"	6'10"	7'0"	7'0"	6'6"	6'8"	7'1"
Height to trolley plank	9'9½"	10'0½"	9'9½"	16'0½"	10'0"	15'7½"	?
Seats total	54	68	62	61	36	76	62
upper deck/lower deck	32/22	34/34	34/28	38/23	36	44/32	40/22
Motors (2 each car)	GE52-4T	GE52-4T	GE52-4T	DK84B	DK30B	DK30B	DK94
Horse-power (nominal)	25	25	25	32	40	40	32
Controllers	BTH	BTH	BTH	DK DB1	DK DB1	DK DB1	DK DB1
	B18	B18	B18	K3	K3	K4	C Spl
Truck	BEC	Brush	BEC	Peckham	Peckham	Brush	Preston
	SB60	Conaty	SB60	P22	P22	MET-type	standard
Wheelbase	6'0"	9'0"	6'0"	8'6"	8'6"	4'6"	7'0"

Key

DD	double-deck	SD	single-deck	OT	open-top
CB	crossbench	OB	open-balcony	TE	totally-enclosed

BEC   The British Electric Car Company Ltd, Trafford Park, Manchester.
Brill   The JG Brill Company, Philadelphia, USA.
BTH   The British Thomson-Houston Company Ltd, Rugby.
DK   Dick, Kerr & Co. Ltd, Preston.
UEC   United Electric Car Co. Ltd, Preston (subsidiary of DK).
EE   The English Electric Co. Ltd, Preston (formed in 1918 by a merger of DK and other companies).

BEC Cars 1 - 30

Typical urban tramcars of the time, these cars were a standard British Electric Car Company design, readily identifiable as such by the corner brackets which incorporated a pattern of four small circles. BEC was a newcomer to tramcar construction, gaining business by undercutting established manufacturers with a price around £350 for each car, but their trams gained a reputation for poor construction, especially with problems originating in the use of unseasoned timber. There were many complaints from operators, and no BEC car survived complete to be kept for preservation. This order for 30 cars was one of the largest received by BEC, and they were the last significant fleet of BEC cars to remain in service anywhere in the country at the end of the Lytham tramways in 1936/7 (probably because many years of seasonal use had reduced their total mileage and allowed plenty of time in the winter for them to be maintained at a noticeably high standard of repair).

The cars were painted royal blue (lined in gold) and cream, the downstairs saloon having wooden longitudinal seats for 22 and windows hung with curtains. Originally there were lattice folding metal gates to the platforms, but

Car No.9 *c.* 1930. *IM Collection*

No.11 at Talbot Square in April 1929. *West Lancashire Evening Gazette*

Above: No.14 after repainting in St Annes Council Tramways livery in 1920. This may have been the first tram to carry the Council livery and lettering. The man standing on the tram step (Mr William Ashton) subsequently became General Manager of the undertaking.   *Official Photograph*

Right: No.17 at Talbot Square *en route* to Lytham, Sunday 6th August, 1933.

M. J. O'Connor

Below: The driver of this BEC car is possibly discussing something with his colleague on Pullman No.47 at Talbot Square in July 1932. Blackpool Dreadnought No.26 behind.

L.A. Gibson

these were soon removed. These cars had quarter-turn reversed stairs to the top deck, an awkward arrangement which restricted the driver's view to the left and gave him something to bang his head on. Upstairs the passengers found a single seat, three double seats, a single seat next to the trolley mast then another four double seats on either side of a centre aisle.

The motors and controllers were durable items found in trams all over Britain, but the SB60 trucks were a British Electric Car Co speciality. Most tramcar trucks incorporated forged or cast sideframes, but the SB60 was assembled from rolled steel sections and angles, with hornways and axlebox springing similar to a railway carriage bogie. It was described as 'light and flexible', but these are not necessarily desirable features in a tramcar truck especially when part of the flexibility comes from leaving the side members unconnected at their outer ends, the truck being held together by the motor suspension beams in the centre. Many operators replaced their BEC trucks, but most of the Lytham ones survived into the 1930s, when it was noticeable how wildly these cars would pitch and sway, but they did go round the sharp curves at Ansdell more easily than the newer long wheelbase cars.

The first 10 trams had arrived by Thursday 21st May, 1903, when No.5 made the first trial run down to Lytham from Squires Gate. After a short time in service advertisements had appeared all round the top deck panels, dash sides and stairs, with a poster board carried in slots at the end of the upper deck canopies.

Nos. 21-30 were soon rebuilt as crossbench cars (see later section) but the other 20 cars changed little in company days, except for the fitting of bigger roller-blind destination boxes and the transfer of the headlamps from a position on the upper deck canopy panelling above the driver's head to the centre of the dash panels, displacing the car fleet number.

After the Council take-over in 1920 the livery became light blue and ivory, the advertisements soon vanished except for the poster boards at either end, and the legend 'St Annes Council Tramways' appeared on the upper deck side panels, to be replaced by 'Lytham St Annes Borough Tramways' after the amalgamation of the towns in 1922.

In March 1927, No.6 was reconditioned to provide an eleventh car for the winter service, with upholstered seats downstairs matching the Pullman cars, a longitudinal double seat in each corner then four transverse single seats one side of the car and four transverse double seats on the other, reducing the saloon seating capacity from 22 to 20. The BEC truck was replaced by a 21E-type truck with Brush sideframes, though it is a little surprising that the original 6ft wheelbase was retained. Subsequently Nos.8 and 15 also received 21E trucks, whilst by May 1928, Nos.9 and 11 had been reconditioned with upholstered seats downstairs but keeping their original trucks. As late as 1936 Nos.6, 9 and 15 had the mesh on the top deck safety rails replaced by panelling.

In company days lack of money was the reason given for not covering the open top decks of these cars, which meant that in bad weather they effectively became 22-seaters. Under the Corporation they soon became seasonal extras, but nevertheless they were plying the 10mile route from Gynn Square to Lytham until they were withdrawn during the last year of the tramways.

No.20 cuts through the sandhills between Squires Gate and St Annes on its way to Lytham in the early years of the century. *IM Collection*

No.10 sits outside Squires Gate Depot in the mid-1930s. The streamlined zig-zag on the dash looks a little incongruous on a 1903 tram virtually in original condition. *K.D. Burton*

A 1 - 20 series car has to wait for a Blackpool 'Balloon' only six months old before it can reverse at Gynn Square in July 1935. *R.B. Parr*

An early view of crossbench No. 33 at St Annes Square. *G.S. Palmer Collection*

NEW OPEN HOLIDAY CARS

FOR THE BLACKPOOL, ST. ANNES & LYTHAM SERVICE.

The new Double Deck Open Car, on the radial truck principle, designed expressly for the Blackpool, St. Annes and Lytham Tramways Company.

The Blackpool, St. Annes and Lytham Electric Tramways Coy. have shown commendable enterprise and consideration for their holiday patrons by providing a number of open cars for the summer traffic. Ten cars, each capable of seating 68 passengers (in and out), have been ordered from the Brush Electrical Engineering Company, and five of them will be running at Whitsuntide. The cars are handsome in design and are built on a new principle, known as the "radial truck," which gives a certain amount of free play in the axle box. It enables the wheel base to be increased from six feet to nine feet, thereby giving a very steady motion to the car and enabling it to get round a sharp curve with ease. Thus the passenger will secure the greatest amount of comfort. In windy or wet weather a strong canvas waterproof screen will cover the car on the weather side. It is only intended to use these cars in fine weather during the summer time. They are, essentially, cars for holiday traffic. The electrical installation is by the British Thompson Houston Company, Rugby.

A contemporary report of the new cars, *St Annes Express*, 9th June, 1905.   *IM Collection*

No.36 in original condition at the Cottage Hospital terminus in 1905.   *IM Collection*

No.31 at St Annes Square in 1932.   *Dr Hugh Nicol*

No.32 looks very new in this view at St Annes Square.   *TD Collection*

Brush crossbench cars 31 - 40

For the start of through running into the centre of Blackpool the company bought these ten cars from Brush of Loughborough, at a price of £520 each, all 10 entering service on Whit Monday, 1905. Designed for summer use only the bottom deck was open-sided, with seven crossbenches each seating four passengers, and a bench seat for three on each of the end platforms. Waterproof oiled canvas curtains were fitted to close the lower deck sides during wet or windy weather (the end bulkheads were glazed). The awkward reversed stairs of the BEC cars were replaced by half-turn direct stairs, but upstairs the seating arrangements were the same, except that the single seat at each end was replaced by a double seat on each end canopy. Unlike the later BEC rebuilds these cars did not have destination boxes, and they had straight-sided bodies and straight edges to the tops of the six open side entrances instead of rounded tops to five side entrances.

The Brush Conaty trucks under these cars were an attempt to produce a long wheelbase truck which would give a smoother ride than the old short trucks, but in which the axles would have a certain amount of flexibilty in their mountings in the rigid truck frame to be able to follow curves more easily. In practice it was found that such trucks worked for a short while when new and well-lubricated, but they soon became rigid by accident or by deliberate modification when worn.

With the few changes already mentioned for the BEC cars these trams lasted until the end of the tramways, presumably not running in traffic again after the end of the Blackpool Illuminations on 19th October, 1936. Whilst none of the Lytham cars were preserved, a ride on a similar design may be enjoyed to this day at Seaton in Devon and one of the original Douglas Head Marine Drive cars is on show at the National Tramway Museum at Crich.

UEC crossbench rebuilds 21 - 30

The Brush crossbench cars were so popular in the summer of 1905 that the following winter BEC cars 21-30 were sent to the Preston works of the United Electric Car Co for rebuilding to a similar configuration, at a cost of £979 2s. 10½d. for all 10. The original four curved corner posts were retained, then new curved intermediate posts were fitted and six crossbenches mounted on the car floor. The saloon doors were replaced by glazed bulkheads, against which there was a full-width seat for five passengers at each end of the car. The other four crossbenches were shorter and only accommodated three passengers, leaving a side aisle so that fares could be collected more safely. A bench on each end platform also accommodated three passengers, whilst the old reversed stairs were replaced by direct stairs leading to seats on the top deck now the same arrangement as the Brush cars.

The history of these cars is similar to that of the Brush crossbench cars, except that it is thought that none was repainted in the zig-zag livery, and No.26 was rebuilt as a single-deck works car in December 1925. The passenger cars last ran in traffic at the end of the Blackpool Illuminations in October 1935, a year ahead

No.35 in the zig-zag livery at Manchester Square on Friday 21st August, 1936. (At least No.31 of this batch was also painted in this livery.) *J.E. Cull*

No.39 by Blackpool Tower in September 1931. *M.J. O'Connor*

In this view No.40 is slightly further down from the Tower.   *TD Collection*

No.22 on Clifton Drive at St Annes Square with the Majestic Hotel in the background.
Dr Hugh Nicol

Turning the trolley on No.29 at Talbot Square, Sunday 6th August, 1933.   *M.J. O'Connor*

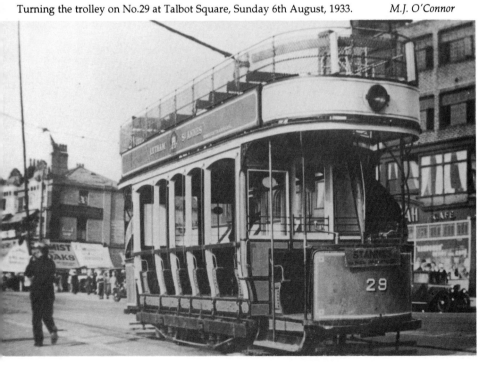

No.26 at Starr Gate in the mid-1930s, running as a works car and painted light grey.
Dr Hugh Nicol/D. W. K. Jones Collection

The bottom deck of No.23 in use as a bus shelter at the Green Drive terminus by Ballam Road in Lytham. It remained in use until it was replaced by a new shelter in 1977. *Alan Judd*

of the Brush cars, but the works car not surprisingly lasted until the end of the tramways in 1937.

Pullman cars 41 - 50

Built to replace the 1903 BEC cars on the basic all-year service these trams were proudly described in the contemporary *Tramway & Railway World*. Modern features included the lightweight high-speed motors, doubly fan ventilated to prevent overheating and enabling 27in. diameter wheels to replace the old 32in. diameter wheels. English Electric papers show that these trams had 71:15 gears:pinions with performance curve 3-84B; the gears on at least some cars (such as No.50) produced a high-pitched whine not unlike the sounds emitted by the Manchester Pilcher four-wheelers. The steel underframe supported teak body pillars and the top deck seats were also wooden, seven double seats on either side of the aisle inside the top-cover and a curved seat for five passengers on each open balcony.

These were the only new trams purchased by Lytham St Annes Corporation, each cost £1,713, made up of £1,050 for the body, £488 for the electrical equipment and £175 for the truck. Seven of the trams arrived in February 1924, and entered service in March; the final three arrived in March and entered service in April. The cost of the purchase was met by a 20-year loan of £17,135.

However, it is a little unfortunate that, with hindsight, it is possible to say that the open ends of these cars contributed to the antiquated image of Lytham St Annes trams in the 1930s. By 1924 many towns were ordering totally-enclosed trams as a matter of course, and whilst the fresh air of the open balconies was attractive to younger passengers the absence of windscreens on such winter cars betrays a lack of concern for the working conditions of motormen. An experimental windscreen was fitted to a Pullman car in June 1935, after the second-hand cars had shown up this deficiency, but the idea was not proceeded with at this late date.

No.42 was carrying lights in support of the Illuminations by 1932, and continued to do so until the end of the 1935 season. All these cars continued in passenger service until the end of the tramways in 1937, when No.41 became the ceremonial last tram on Wednesday 28th April. The others were dismantled in 1937 but No.41 was kept in Squires Gate Depot until it was broken up for the war effort in 1943.

The lower deck of No.43 was discovered in the early 1970s and taken to the West Lancashire Light Railway at Alty's brickworks, Hesketh Bank (between Preston and Southport). For several years it was used as a mess room, but preservation attempts failed and in the early 1990s the body was dismantled for possible use as a railway coach, the two body sides at present hanging on a wall inside a shed.

Dearne District cars 51 - 54

Originally four of the initial batch of 25 cars built by English Electric in 1924 for the Dearne District Light Railways in South Yorkshire, these were fast,

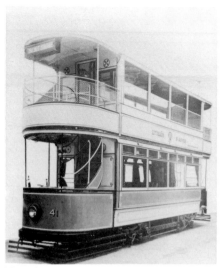

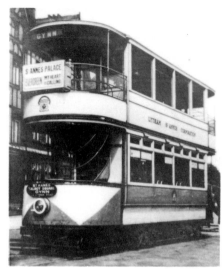

No.41 brand new.   *Official photograph*

A Pullman car in the zig-zag livery at the Lytham terminus (the Gynn via Lytham Road route board is hiding the fleet number).
JG Collection

The destination 'East Beach' dates this view of No.43 before the abandonment of the line to the Cottage Hospital in July 1926.
IM Collection

The conductor is about to turn the trolley pole on No.45 at Gynn Square in Blackpool, before returning to Lytham via the Pleasure Beach and South Promenade, in 1934. *TD Collection*

The sumptuous bottom deck of No.41. *Official photograph*

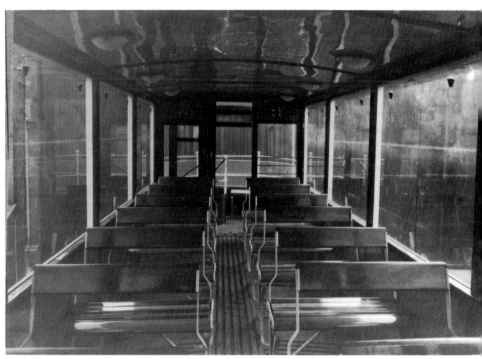

The more spartan wooden seats on the top deck of No.41. *Official photograph*

No.42 when running as an illuminated car. *JG Collection*

A slight blur shows that the motorman is spinning the handbrake off before driving No.43 away from Talbot Square in Blackpool. *IM Collection*

No.44 unusually has the legend 'Lytham St Annes Corporation' immediately below the upper deck windows. *JG Collection*

No.46 passes open-topper No.20. *JG Collection*

No.47 shows its lighting arrangements at dusk. *JG Collection*

A subsequent view of No.47 in daylight (6th August, 1933), with no Corporation title along the top deck panels and the crest halfway along the waist panel.   *R. Elliott*

No.48 in the zig-zag livery is about to return from St Annes Square to the Gynn on 8th April, 1937, in the last month of operation.   *H.B. Priestley*

No.49 in Lytham, 7th August, 1934.   *S.L. Smith*

When the driver appears No.50 will return to the Gynn via St Annes and Lytham Road.

R. Wilson

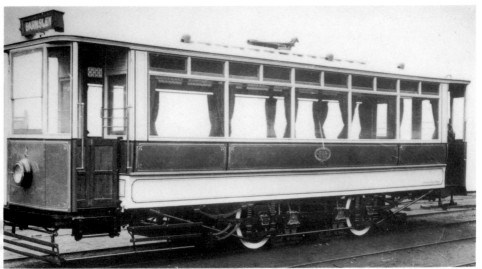

Top: An official view of Dearne District No.1 when new. *P.H. Abell Collection*

Centre: The scenery of Wath-on-Dearne could hardly have been more different from the Fylde: Dearne District No.30 of the second batch climbs Burman Road on its way to the Woodman.
P.H. Abell Collection

Right: No.51 stands by the North Pier at Blackpool (Talbot Square) in 1934.
H.A. Whitcombe/Science Museum

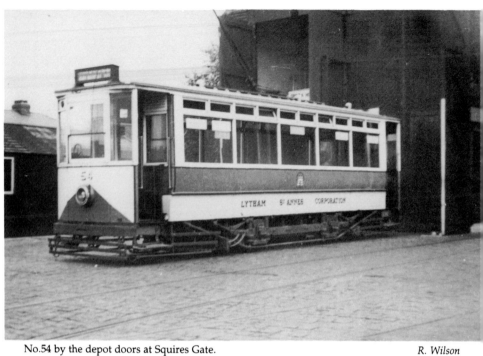

No.54 by the depot doors at Squires Gate.   *R. Wilson*

An official photograph of No. 55 as Accrington No.39.   *TD Collection*

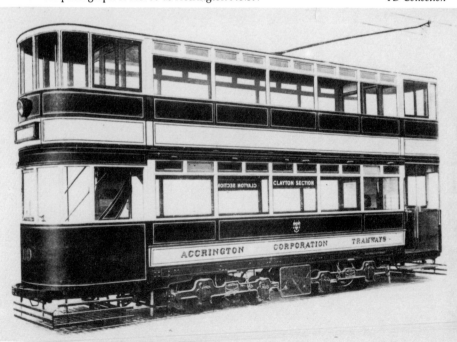

No.55 'Big Bertha' running through the sandhills towards Blackpool *c.*1936.　　　　　*F. Dean*

No.55 at Talbot Square in 1937. Blackpool No.256 to the right is still running as No.719.
Dennis Gill Collection

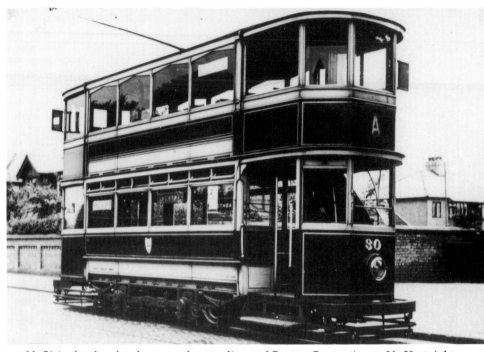

No.56 in the chocolate brown and cream livery of Preston Corporation as No.30 at Ashton terminus on 29th June, 1934. *R. Elliott*

No.56 approaches the original gas tram terminus on Lytham Road opposite the junction with Station Road *c.* 1936. *K.D. Burton*

roomy single-deckers only marred by their wooden seats (longitudinal seats for 18 each side of the saloon). Lytham St Annes bought them for winter use in 1933, paying £500 for the lot and repainting them in the zig-zag livery of bright blue and brilliant white, with red lead truck, fenders and lifeguards.

During the winter of 1933/4 they operated on the Lytham-Gynn Square service but Walter Luff, General Manager of Blackpool Corporation Tramways, objected to their small carrying capacity [sic] and they were subsequently restricted to local services within Lytham St Annes, such as the Queen Mary School specials with 'Balmoral Road' or 'Highbury Road' on the destination blind. They were withdrawn and scrapped in 1937.

Accrington car 55

One of a pair built by Brush in 1915, this was No.39 when the Accrington tramways closed in January 1932. The following year it went to Lytham St Annes for trials, being regauged to standard gauge from the Accrington gauge of 4ft and gaining DK30B motors instead of its original DK11D pair. A long totally-enclosed car, the only bogie tram in the Lytham fleet, it had longitudinal seating for 32 passengers downstairs and transverse wooden garden seats upstairs (double seats on one side and single on the other), with a curved seat in each enclosed balcony.

The Brush bogies were of the maximum traction type, and were basically similar to a design previously supplied to the Metropolitan Electric Tramways in North London. Each bogie had an outer pair of 32in. diameter wheels driven by the motor and an inner pair of 22in. diameter pony wheels, giving the smooth riding of a bogie car whilst only using two motors for economy, and yet deriving the maximum traction from them since around 80 per cent of the weight of the tram was being carried by the driven wheels. Unfortunately the pony wheels of maximum traction bogies were prone to derailment, and the regauging perhaps did not help matters. Nicknamed Big Bertha, or Waltzing Matilda, No.55 became notorious for coming off the track, most commonly on the tight curves near the White Church and the railway footbridge on Ansdell Road South, so eventually it was restricted to working Woodlands Road turn-backs, which was something of a pity as it was very steady on straight track if a little slow compared with the Pullman cars. The car survived until the end of the tramways in 1937, but the other three cars which Accrington was saving for Lytham went to Southend-on-Sea instead.

Preston car 56

Originally Preston No.30 this was one of three hybrid trams (30,40 and 42) built by Preston Corporation Tramways in their own workshops in the late 1920s for the Ashton route, which had a very low railway bridge on Fylde Road. The bottom deck incorporated parts from one of Preston's original 1904 trams (12, 13, 18 or 22), reposted from three to four windows, and the top deck incorporated parts of an even older single-decker bought from Sheffield in 1918

(40 or 42) shortened from five to four windows. This produced a speedy tram with upholstered seats throughout: longitudinal seats for 22 downstairs and 10 double seats on each side upstairs.

Sold to Lytham St Annes Corporation it travelled to Squires Gate Depot by road through Lytham on a low-loader, arriving on Monday 27th August, 1934. It is thought that it actually ran for a short time in the dark red Preston livery, before being repainted in the zig-zag Lytham colours, the only other change being the fitting of a roller destination blind to replace the original Preston route letter box.

A little surprisingly this was the only tram in Lytham fitted with quarter-turn direct-stairs to the top deck, the original BEC cars having reversed stairs which led passengers behind the driver (but gave him something to bang his head on and restricted his view to the left) and the crossbench cars and the Pullmans having half-turn direct stairs.

Unfortunately it was mounted on a four-wheel truck of only 7ft wheelbase, hardly longer than the BEC cars of 1903, and it reportedly pitched and swayed violently like a BEC car on the journey from the Gynn to Lytham. Nevertheless this car too survived until the end of the Lytham tramways in 1937.

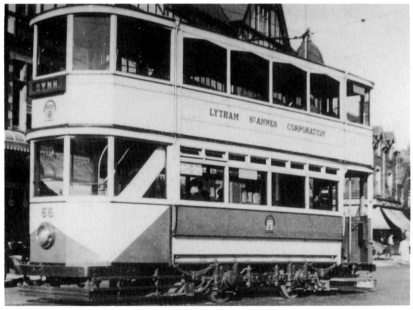

No.56 at the Lytham terminus *c.* 1936. The roller destination blind was fitted on its arrival on the Lytham system in 1934.   *R. Wilson*

Along the Routes in Pictures
Squires Gate-Lytham Cottage Hospital (East Beach)
Stony Hill Bridge

Lytham Pullman No.43 *c*. 1927 on the earlier railway bridge, over which the tracks were laid too close for trams to pass each other. *Frank Dean*

A view towards Starr Gate as Pullman No.42 climbs over the bridge *c*. 1927. Note the large banner 'Stand here for Lytham St Annes trams'. The cottages on the left were demolished in the late 1950s. *Blackpool Historical Society*

Through the Sandhills

A Brush crossbench car leads a BEC car at Starr Gate as they approach the right-angle turn into Squires Gate Lane on the way to Blackpool in company days. This is now the junction for the road into Blackpool via South Promenade. *TD Collection*

Tram No.16 on its way to Lytham passes No.11 at Starr Gate. The tracks along Squires Gate Lane can be seen in the background. *IM Collection*

An open-top tram emerging from sandhills. *A. Stevenson Collection*

A nanny attends to her charge as No.5 passes by.   *IM Collection*

No.8 races a bicycle through the sandhills as it approaches the outskirts of St Annes on Sea.
IM Collection

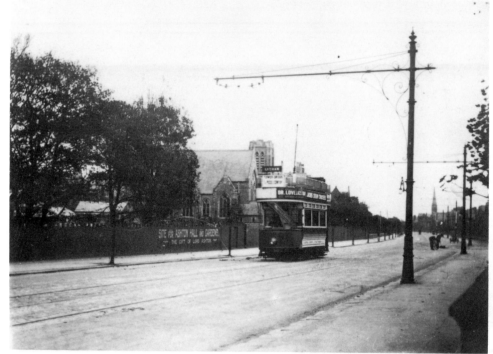

Tram No.7 passes St George's Garden (now Ashton Gardens) in 1914. St Annes Congregational Church is in the background.   *Frank Dean*

Open-sided crossbench tram No.40 at St Annes Square *c.* 1930 with the Congregational Church and Ashton Gardens in the background.   *TD Collection*

No. 5 stands at the passenger shelter at St Annes Square, *en route* to Lytham in August 1929.
G.S. Palmer Collection

Company trams at St Annes Square *c.* 1903 looking towards Clifton Drive South. *IM Collection*

St Annes on Sea.   Clifton Drive.

Built in 1909 and demolished in 1975, the Imperial Hydro was the largest and most luxurious hotel in St Annes with 200 bedrooms and a ballroom. It was renamed the Majestic Hotel in 1920 and in 1948 Winston Churchill stayed there during the Conservative Party Conference.

Saidman Bros

A view across the shale tennis courts of the Majestic Hotel as tram No.9 passes St Annes Square in the late 1920s. This land is now occupied by 'The Admiral' public house.

Frank Dean Collection

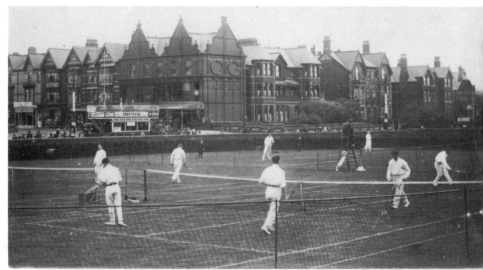

A group of pedestrians are standing in the road chatting alongside No.17, and a boy with a tricycle looks on. *Stuart Ibbotson Collection*

In the mid-1930s tram No.31 is being pursued by a motor van past the traffic lights at St Annes Square in this busy tramway scene. *S.L. Smith*

Clifton Drive South, Lytham St Annes

The photographer of tram No.7 is watched by a postman in front of St Annes Post Office.

T. Morris Collection

Company car No.5 passes The Drive Methodist Church (near Astland Street) on its way to Blackpool.

IM Collection

Heading north to Gynn Square No.13 passes St Thomas's Church *c.* 1930.

JG Collection

Fairhaven and Ansdell

Playing golf on the old Fairhaven course, now the grounds of Queen Mary School.

Frank Dean Collection

No.15 *en route* to Lytham at Fairhaven tram shelter. Until recently, buses still used this stop. The shelter is still kept in an excellent condition, complete with hanging flower baskets in the summer months. A well known landmark 'The White Church' can be seen in the background, it is at that point the tramway turned left 90 degrees into Ansdell Road South.

G.S. Palmer Collection

No.47 rounds the corner from Ansdell Road South into Cambridge Road on its way to Lytham on 15th December, 1936, the last day of tram services on this section, with the footbridge over the railway in the background.   *Frank Dickinson*

Heading for Central station in Blackpool, tram No.10 travels along Cambridge Road parallel to the railway near Stanley Road *c.* 1908.   *IM Collection*

Approaching Lytham

Right: On the single track section in Church Road No.7 passes Lowther Gardens *c.* 1920.
IM Collection

Centre: No.15 approaches Lowther Terrace tram stop on a short working to St Annes *c.* 1908.
P. Carr Collection

Bottom: A view of Clifton Square looking along Dicconson Terrace *c.* 1900 showing gas trams 17 and 12.
JG Collection

Clifton Square, Lytham

Above: An early view of a Company tram in Clifton Square. Note the tracks in the foreground, from which a single line ran to the former Henry Street gas tram depot.
IM Collection

Centre: No.1 waits to depart for Blackpool.
IM Collection

Below: Thirty years later tram No.41 repeats the above scene.
R. Wilson

Crossbench tram No.35 enters the square while Pullman No.41 loads for Blackpool in 1925.
Dennis Gill Collection

By the 1950s the former traction poles were being used for street lighting and the service to St. Annes is provided by Lytham St Annes Corporation bus No.18 (GTB 905), a Leyland PD1 new in 1946 and withdrawn from service in 1970.　　　　　*West Lancashire Evening Gazette*

Towards the Cottage Hospital

Top: No.4 leaves Clifton Square for the short journey along Clifton Street and Warton Street to the Cottage Hospital (East Beach). The Talbot Hotel can be seen on the left. *IM Collection*

Centre: No.11 passing the Lytham Institute in Warton Street, built in 1878 and now in use as Lytham Library. *IM Collection*

Left: No.8 stands at the Cottage Hospital terminus (tram services ceased on the line out from Lytham Square on Friday 23rd July, 1926). *TD Collection*

Blackpool Promenade (Gynn Square - Starr Gate)
Gynn Square

Gynn Square in the late 1920s with Lytham No.8 beside Blackpool Dreadnought No.61, and Lytham No.3 reversing over the crossover to follow No.8 back past the Tower. The third track was laid in 1924, whilst the Lytham tram service was extended a mile northwards from Talbot Square to the Gynn on 23rd July, 1926. *Saidman Bros*

No.14 leaves Gynn Square for Lytham one morning in August 1928. The Blackpool trams in the background include double-deck standard No.40, now preserved at the National Tramway Museum, Crich. *JG Collection*

North Promenade

No.12 picks its way over track repairs near the Imperial Hotel. *National Tramway Museum*

Central Promenade

Lytham crossbench car No.33 heads north from Central Pier *c.* 1930. Note the absence of Woolworths in front of the Tower: this was built in 1936. *Saidman Bros*

The small destination board on the dash hides the identity of this Pullman passing the Foxhall Hotel c. 1935.   *T. Morris Collection*

Blackpool Corporation bought the Brush cars in 1937 partly to fill the gap left by the withdrawal of the Lytham tram services. No.632, passing the Foxhall in May 1977, is still in traffic, but the historic public house has since been demolished.   *Jim Ingham*

Pleasure Beach

Top: A busy scene just north of the Pleasure Beach *c.* 1936 with two Lytham open-toppers surrounded by a variety of Blackpool trams. The nearer Lytham car (No.9) has had its top deck panelling raised to make it less draughty, as did Nos.6 and 15 also - perhaps this did not make them look quite so antiquated beside the new Blackpool streamliners. *JG Collection*

Centre: A pair of 1934 railcoaches contrast with Lytham No.10 of 1903 at the Pleasure Beach terminus. *JG Collection*

Left: A Blackpool 'open boat' uses the 1928 link line from the Promenade tracks to Squires Gate Lane. Tarred over for many years the eastbound track was uncovered in July 1957, and put into use again for these circular tours. *D. Tate*

Blackpool Central Station

Lytham crossbench cars including No.32 lined up in Hounds Hill alongside the Palatine Hotel
c. 1907.   *Dennis Gill Collection*

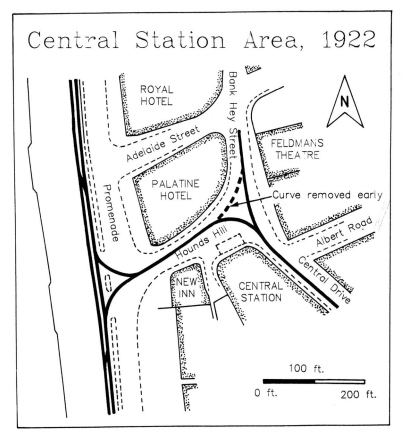

Central Station Area, 1922

ROYAL HOTEL

Bank Hey Street

FELDMANS THEATRE

Adelaide Street

PALATINE HOTEL

Promenade

Curve removed early

Albert Road

Hounds Hill

Central Drive

NEW INN

CENTRAL STATION

N

100 ft.

0 ft.   200 ft.

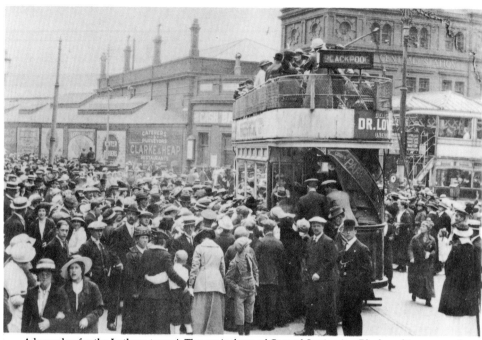

A busy day for the Lytham trams! The car in front of Central Station is a Blackpool top-covered Motherwell.

JG Collection

Central Drive

Blackpool No.45, a top-covered Motherwell car originally built as an open-topper by Hurst Nelson in 1902, heads out of town along Central Drive. At Waterloo Road it will turn left to reach Marton, but between 1905 and 1923 Lytham trams turned right along Waterloo Road then left at the Royal Oak to run along Lytham Road to Squires Gate. Note the unusual short bracket arms supporting the overhead wires at the side of the road. The photograph shows Central Drive at its junction with Rigby Road: at this point the Spen Dyke passes under the road as it flows from Marton Moss to the sea at Manchester Square, and after heavy rain it tended to flood. This was the scene on Friday 1st September, 1922, a day on which three inches of rain fell.

IM Collection

Lytham Road

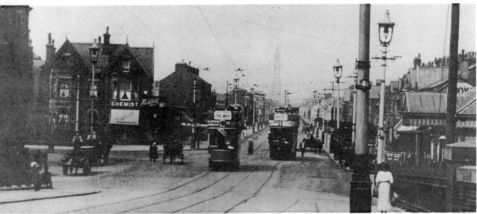

Top: South Shore railway station (opposite Station Road) was the terminus of the Lytham tramway from July 1896, to July 1905. The station itself was closed on 14th July, 1916, when the station at Waterloo Road (now Blackpool South) was extended, but the original station buildings from South Shore were rebuilt as semi-detached bungalows on Rough Heys Lane (off Common Edge Road in Marton) and are still in use today. Open-top trams 11 and 16 pass the station entrance with Skew Bridge in the background. *IM Collection*

Centre: A view northwards from the top of Skew Bridge with tram No.7 heading towards Blackpool town centre. *JG Collection*

Right: Looking south as No.4 climbs the upgrade over Skew Bridge. *IM Collection*

Top: A Lytham tram disappears over Skew Bridge on its way to Blackpool.
Jim Ingham Collection

Left: No.6 heads out of Blackpool along Lytham Road near Watson Road.
IM Collection

Below: Blackpool-bound No.12 approaches Highfield Road in Company days.
IM Collection

Blackpool Pantograph No.169 by the same location as No.12 (*previous page*) half a century later on an enthusiasts' tour.
Robert F. Mack

A vintage scene outside Arnold School opposite Roseberry Avenue: a Crown Laundry van overtakes tram No.9 underneath a lovely set of bracket arms and finials on the traction poles; tram No.10 behind.
Oakley of St Annes on Sea

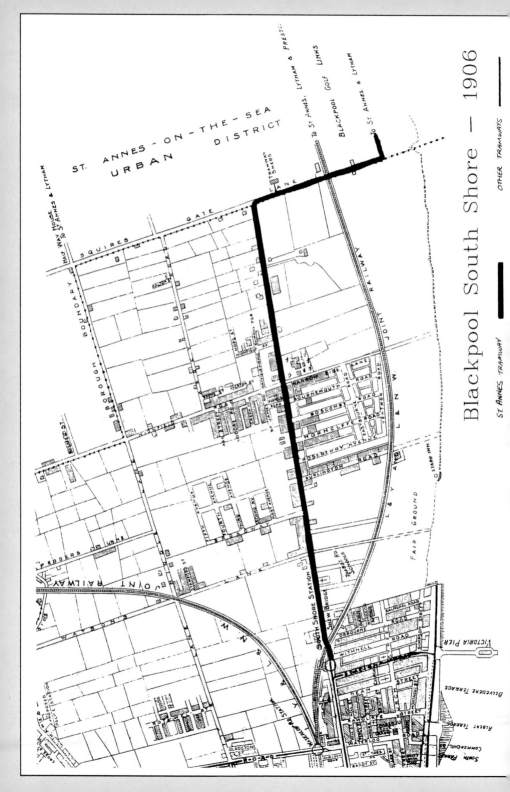

Blackpool South Shore — 1906

ST. ANNES TRAMWAY ——— OTHER TRAMWAYS

Blackpool Tram Tours on Squires Gate Lane

Right: Former open-topper No.244 (now No.707) heads east towards the junction with Lytham Road, where a railcoach is waiting to depart from the terminus on Saturday 23rd May, 1959. *R.B. Parr*

Centre: Trailer towing car No.275 passes the former Lytham St Annes tram depot in 1960. The partly tarred-over tracks leading to the depot fan are still *in situ*. Squires Gate Station in the background opened on 14th September, 1931. *Graham Weaver*

Bottom: Formerly Stony Hill Bridge, Squires Gate Bridge was rebuilt in 1931. Standards Nos.40 and 41 wait for photographers on Sunday 22nd June, 1958. *IM Collection*

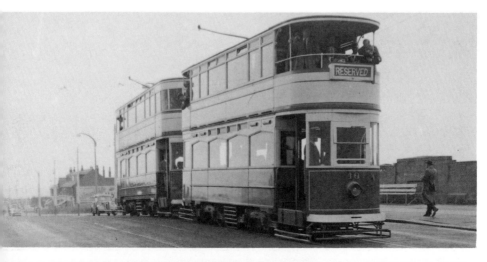

LYTHAM ROAD GAS TRAM DEPOT – 1900

stream

Lytham Road

A

B

Squires Gate Lane

Fold Lane

It is thought that building 'B' is the running shed because of the large space in front of the building giving room for a track fan to the various depot roads, leaving building 'A' as the compressor house, stores and manager's office.

N

Scale 1: 3,125
Scale 1: 2500

LYTHAM TOWN CENTRE – 1908
SHOWING THE EX. GAS TRAM DEPOT

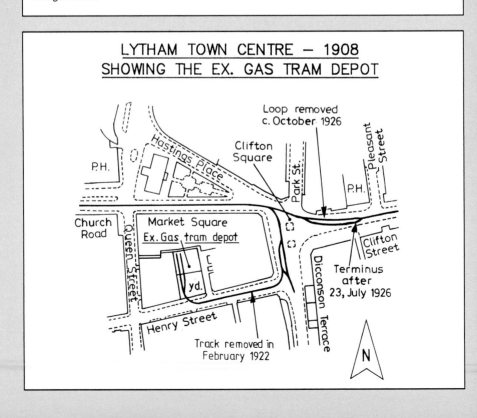

Loop removed
c. October 1926

Clifton
Square

Hastings Place

Pleasant Street

Park St.

P.H.

P.H.

Church
Road

Market Square
Ex. Gas tram depot

Queen Street

Clifton
Street

Terminus
after
23, July 1926

Dicconson Terrace

yd.

Henry Street

Track removed in
February 1922

N

Chapter Four

Operating Details

Henry Street Depot, Lytham

A small gas tram depot in the centre of Lytham, this building had previously been used as a roller-skating rink. In 1896 it was converted into a two-road depot to house gas trams, being reached by a single-track along Henry Street which turned sharp right into the depot yard then branched into the two tracks before entering the depot. On the night of the storm which wrecked the main depot in Lytham Road in 1903, this depot was accommodating seven gas trams, but it was never converted for electric operation, and by 1911 the building was in use as the Lytham Picture House cinema. Later it housed auctioneers, then it became a small engineering workshop and garage before being demolished with some of the surrounding area around 1986. Sheltered accommodation called 'The Homestead' has now been built on the site. The track along Henry Street to the depot was removed in February 1922.

Stony Hill Depot 1896-1900

This was the company's first depot, located just within the district of St Annes, on the site of the present Squires Gate bus depot. Unfortunately we have found no photographs, maps or diagrams of the depot, but it is known that it had at least two tracks which both came off the main line on Fold Lane (now Squires Gate Lane) from the Blackpool direction. During the period of horse car operation the horses were stabled at this depot.

Lytham Road Depot 1900-1903

Because the price of gas in Blackpool was considerably less than that charged by the St Annes Gas Co. it was decided to build a new depot on the Blackpool side of the boundary. This was a spacious depot, with a gas compressor house, stores and manager's office alongside the running shed. Again we have been unable to find any photographs, maps or diagrams of this depot except for a close-up of gas tram 16 with the depot buildings in the background. The running shed (offset from the other building) seemed a well-built brick structure with a corrugated-iron roof, until it was practically razed to the ground at 6.30 am on Friday 27th February, 1903, when it is thought that the south wall of the shed collapsed in strong gales. This brought down the rest of the building on top of the 13 trams inside at the time. Damage was estimated at £2,000, excluding the loss of 10 trams which were damaged beyond repair. The rest of the buildings were virtually undamaged, but the gas trams never ran in public service again, and the tramway did not reopen until electrification was completed. The site is now occupied by houses 670-678 Lytham Road.

SEND YOUR LOCAL PARCELS

BY THE

Tramways Parcels Express

Parcels may be given to the Conductor on any car, or same may be handed in to the Tramways Parcels Receiving Offices, viz.:—

Mr. A. BROWN, Tobacconist, 4, Station Buildings, Lytham Rd., South Shore.

Mr. CHADWICK, Tobacconist, 47, The Square, St. Annes.

Mr. J. CROWTHER, Stationer, 70, Clifton Street, Lytham.

Blackpool, St. Annes, & Lytham Tramways Co. LTD.

Every effort will be made to ensure the punctual running of Cars in accordance with this Time Table, but at night, owing to the lighting restrictions, it may be extremely difficult to run to the times stated, the policy of the management being "safely before punctuality," and the Company will not hold themselves responsible for any delay which may occur.

H. W. LAING, General Manager.

Oct., 1916.

Blackpool, St. Annes, and Lytham Tramways Co., Ltd.

General Manager: H. W. LAING. Offices: Squires Gate, Blackpool.

TIME TABLE

Telephone 327.

Blackpool, St. Annes, and Lytham Tramways Co., Ltd.

General Manager: H. W. LAING. Offices: Squires Gate, Blackpool.

TIME TABLE

Telephone 327.

IMPORTANT.

In case any Passenger should have cause for complaint in regard to irregularity or incivility on the part of any of the Company's Servants, it is requested that the complaint should be made in writing to the General Manager, Squires Gate, Blackpool, and that the number of the Car, together with the time or the ticket issued by the Conductor, or the Conductor's number, should be given in the letter of complaint.

Private Cars can be obtained for special parties. Terms for these can be obtained on application to the General Manager.

Passengers are requested to see that they receive a correct ticket for the fare paid, and the ticket should be punched in their presence.

Each Passenger should show his ticket when requested to do so, to the Conductor, or to any duly authorised Servant of the Company, and also when required deliver up his ticket.

Cars will stop to pick up and set down Passengers at the fixed Stopping Places only, and Passengers joining or leaving a Car between these places, or while the Car is in motion, do so at their own risk.

No Passenger will be permitted to travel on the steps or platform of any Car, and any person so travelling shall cease to do so when requested by any of the Company's Officials.

Secretaries of Clubs, organisers of concerts, or other public meetings, are asked to notify the General Manager of any special meetings, when, if the traffic warrants it, extra Cars will be run.

BLACKPOOL TO LYTHAM.

Stations:

- Central Station
- Waterloo Hotel
- Dunes Hotel
- Depot
- Manchester C. Home
- St. Annes Road West
- Balmoral Road
- Woodlands Road
- Lytham Square
- Cottage Hospital Arr.

And every 10 mins.

a Sundays excepted. * Sundays only.

LYTHAM TO BLACKPOOL.

Stations:

- Cottage Hospital
- Lytham Square
- Woodlands Road
- St. Annes Road West
- Manchester C. Home
- Depot
- Dunes Hotel
- South Shore
- Waterloo Hotel
- Central Station Arr.

And every 10 mins.

Lytham St. Annes Borough Tramways.

TRAMWAY
AND
BUS
SERVICES

TELEPHONE Nos. 244 and 2245 BLACKPOOL.

H. W. LAING, Gen. Manager.

Squires Gate,
Blackpool.

October, 1928.

"Lytham St. Annes Express," St. Annse-on-Sea.

EVERY effort will be made to ensure the punctual running of Trams and Motor Buses in accordance with this time-table, but the service cannot be guaranteed, and the Corporation will not hold themselves responsible for any delays which may occur.

Each passenger shall show his ticket, when requested to do so, to the driver, conductor, or to any duly authorised servant of the Corporation, and also when required, deliver up his ticket.

H. W. LAING,
General Manager.

Tramway Offices,
Squires Gate, Blackpool.

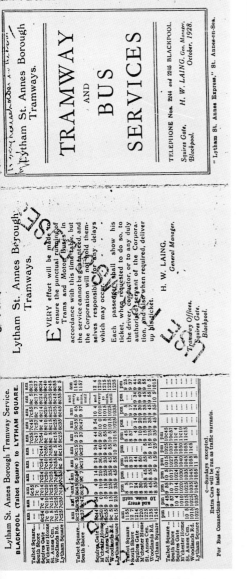

Lytham St. Annes Borough Tramway Service.
BLACKPOOL (Talbot Square) to LYTHAM SQUARE.

Talbot Square, South Shore, Squires Gate, St. Annes Cen., M'chester Home, Woodlands Rd., Lytham Square.

c—Sundays excepted.

Extra Cars will be run as traffic warrants.

For Bus Connections—see inside.

LYTHAM SQUARE to BLACKPOOL (Talbot Square).

Lytham Square, Woodlands Rd., St. Annes Cen., Squires Gate, South Shore, Talbot Square.

c—Sundays excepted. Extra Cars will be run as traffic warrants.

[10 minutes until and every 10 minutes]

For Bus Connections—see inside.

ROUTE No. 1a.—ST. ANNES CENTRE and ALBERT ROAD.

Albert Road ...... dept.
St. Annes Centre ...... arr.
Albert Road ...... arr.

and every 20 minutes until

c—Sundays excepted.

Route No. 3 Buses connect with Trams at St. Annes Centre, at 6, 15, 25, 35, 45 and 55 minutes past the hour.
Route No. 1a Buses connect with Trams at 5, 15, 35 and 55 minutes past the hour.

ROUTE No. 3.—ST. ANNES CENTRE and LEACH LANE via ST. DAVID'S ROAD.

Leach Lane ...... dept.
St. Annes Centre ...... arr.
Leach Lane ...... arr.

and every 10 minutes

Trams connect with Buses to Green Drive at Lytham Square, at 5, 25, 45 and 55 minutes past the hour.
Buses from Green Drive connect with Trams at Lytham Square.
All Buses on Meadow Lane (No. 5) Route connect with Trams at Lytham Square.

Extra Buses will be run as traffic warrants.

ROUTE No. 4.—ST. ANNES, LYTHAM and GREEN DRIVE.

ST. ANNES to LYTHAM:—
St. Annes Centre ...... dept.
Eastgate ...... "
Woodlands Road ...... "
Lytham Square ...... "
Green Drive ...... arr.

LYTHAM to ST. ANNES:—
Green Drive ...... dept.
Lytham Square ...... "
Woodlands Road ...... "
Eastgate ...... "
St. Annes Centre ...... arr.

and every 20 minutes until

c—Sundays excepted.

ROUTE No. 5.—LYTHAM SQUARE and MEADOW LANE.

Lytham Square ...... dept.
Meadow Lane ...... "
Lytham Square ...... arr.

and every 20 minutes until

c—Sundays excepted.

Note Tram Connections.

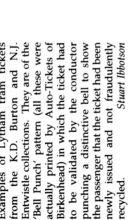

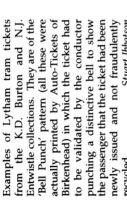

Examples of Lytham tram tickets from the K.D. Burton and N.J. Entwistle collections. They are of the 'Bell Punch' pattern (all these were actually printed by Auto-Tickets of Birkenhead) in which the ticket had to be validated by the conductor punching a distinctive bell to show the passenger that the ticket had been newly issued and not fraudulently recycled.   *Stuart Ibbotson*

An exuberant poster from pre-1914. There is an implication that the Tramways Company is encouraging passengers (from Blackpool) to travel through to Lytham rather than leave the car at St Annes.

Squires Gate Depot 1903-date

For the electrification of the line, and following the collapse of the gas tram depot, a third new depot was constructed in 1903-04, on the site of the original 1896 Stony Hill depot.

The work was commenced in 1903, but the eight-track depot was not officially opened until June 1904. Until the building had been completed the new electric cars Nos. 1-20, which were built for the reopening of the line, were kept at a 'temporary depot' thought to be the site of the former gas tram depot on Lytham Road, but it is also known that while construction work took place trams were parked up along Fold Lane (Squires Gate Lane) at night with their lights on.

The most adventurous trips undertaken by Lytham trams were performed at the end of the 1903 summer season when five cars went for storage in Copse Road Depot in Fleetwood, presumably because the Lytham manager was a friend of the Camerons on the Blackpool & Fleetwood Tramroad. They made the journey on the night of 16th-17th October, and most became derailed at the old Rossall Curve (since replaced by a straighter section of line), where the narrower tyres of the Lytham trams could not cope with the spread of the ungrooved tramroad track. The cars returned on 16th May, 1904, and since there were at that time no physical connections onto the Blackpool Corporation tracks at the Gynn and South Shore they must have been dragged over the gaps at those places.

The depot originally had offices and a store at the rear of tracks 5-8 (the half of the building towards the sea), next to a machine shop with a smithy fire at the rear of tracks 1-4. In 1910 an eight-track workshop extension at the rear of the depot gave much improved facilities: a workshop, paintshop, office, machine shop, smiths shop and store. The following year handsome bungalow-style offices were built in front of the depot, set off by flower gardens and rockeries. This building replaced the offices at 300 Lytham Road, and included a ticket office, general office and advertising office on the ground floor, with two ticket stores and a men's room above them.

Work started in July 1923, on a new four-track depot extension on the east side of the existing depot to house the new Pullman trams (41-50) which were on order. Formally opened on Wednesday 12th March, 1924, at a cost of £8,111, this extension was divided by hinged doors into a running shed for trams in service at the front, and a new spacious paintshop with a wood block floor behind. After the tramway system closed down in April 1937, the four tracks in the 1924 extension were retained at the request of Blackpool Corporation for the possible dispersal of their tram fleet in the event of a war, though in fact the overhead wires in the yard and the depot were taken down and the emergency measures were never used.

It is a strange fact that for many years the freehold of the former Lytham St Annes bus depot has been owned by Blackpool Corporation despite the land involved being outside the Blackpool boundary - this situation arose out of an opportunist purchase from the Clifton Estate.

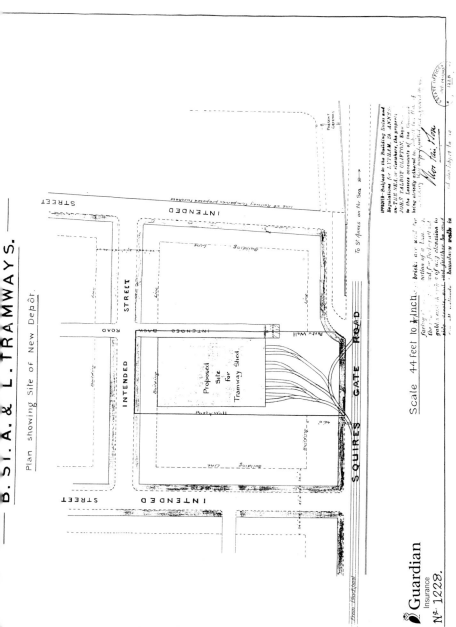

B. St. A. & L. TRAMWAYS.

Plan showing Site of New Depôt.

STREET
INTENDED

STREET
INTENDED

INTENDED BACK ROAD

STREET
INTENDED

Proposed Site for Tramway Shed

Party Wall

Line of Railway Companies proposed Purchase

SQUIRES GATE ROAD

To St. Annes on the Sea →

From Blackpool

Scale 44 feet to 1 Inch.

Guardian
Insurance
No. 1228.

An original plan for the Squires Gate Depot. When completed the track layout into 'Squires Gate Road' was slightly different, and the 'Intended Street' at the back of the depot became workshops and yard.

Guardian Insurance

Squires Gate Depot *c.* 1906 in original condition clearly showing the depot fan leading to eight tracks, with trams from the 1-20 and 21-30 classes visible inside.   *IM Collection*

An excellent interior view of Squires Gate Depot *c.* 1906, showing crossbench trams from the 31-40 class in original condition, and one of the 1906 rebuilds, No.24.   *Blackpool Historical Society*

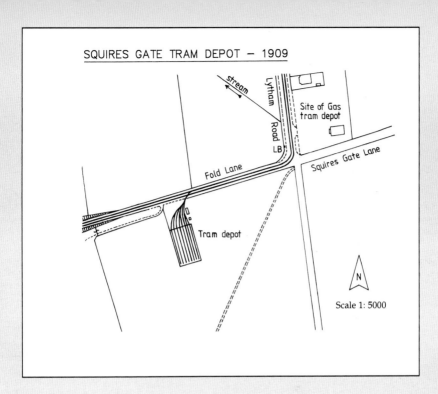

SQUIRES GATE TRAM DEPOT — 1909

stream
Lytham Road
Site of Gas tram depot
Squires Gate Lane
LB
Fold Lane
Tram depot
N
Scale 1: 5000

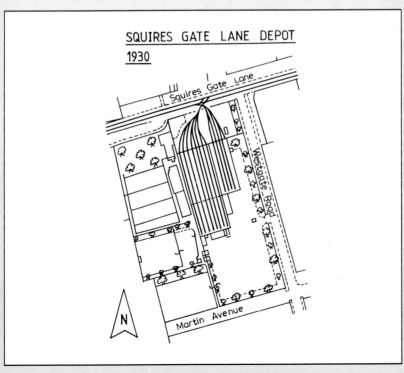

SQUIRES GATE LANE DEPOT
1930

Squires Gate Lane
Westgate Road
Martin Avenue
N

The 8-track workshop extension seen in 1976. *Garth Harper*

A front view of Squires Gate Depot showing how well the 1924 extension on the left blends in with the original depot built 20 years earlier. This view in the mid-1930s shows trams in the zig-zag livery introduced in 1932. *R. Elliott*

The workshops in the mid-1970s, still with tram rails either side of the inspection pit. Bus No. 50 was one of six Seddon RU 6LX chassis with Pennine B47D bodies which entered service in October 1972. It was rebuilt to B51F condition in May 1981, but withdrawn a year later.

Garth Harper

St Thomas Road Sub-station

The Tramway Company's sub-station (which was supplied with electricity by the St Annes UDC generating station) was built in St Thomas Road, St Annes. From this building electricity was distributed both for traction and lighting along the entire route. The sub-station was given the aspect of a private house and even a house number, 24. It is quite a handsome building and still adds dignity to the residential area surrounding it.

The building was so arranged that the batteries and other equipment lay underground at the front of the 'house', but were conveniently at ground level at the back. There were 2 boosters and a 700 Amp hour battery of 240 cells to give 500 volts traction supply. The battery was supplied by the Accumulator Industry Co. Ltd of Woking, and the switchboard, reversible and direct boosters by Crompton & Co. of Chelmsford and London. The electric cables were supplied by the Anchor Cable Co. of Leigh, Lancashire, laid in earthenware troughs filled with bitumen, with the UDC cables entering one side of the building and the Tramway Company's supply cables leaving the other side. Above the electrical equipment there were four well-arranged rooms which were used as a private residence at a yearly rent of £22 around 1935.

The whole of the building is now in use as a private residence, 'St Thomas Court', with the date 1903 still clearly visible above the front door.

In 1912 the method of working the sub-station was described in detail in an issue of the tramway magazine. Overnight and in the early morning the electricity supply was all from the battery cells, and this arrangement powered the tramway until traffic increased after 9 o'clock. By then the load might have touched 180 amps, reducing the line voltage from 500 to 490 volts once or twice, and it would be time to ring the signal bell to the St Annes UDC generating station (the 'Light Works') for them to share the load for the rest of the day.

A dozen trams on the circuit between Squires Gate and Lytham could produce a momentary current demand as high as 390 amps if four of them were starting off at the same time (taking a current of 60 amps each). In these circumstances a steady supply of 180 amps from the Light Works would mean that the battery would have to supply the other 210 amps. On the other hand if some of the cars should then coast with power off, or come to stops, the load could drop to 100 amps. The 180 amps from the Light Works would then supply the 100 amps load and leave 80 amps to charge the battery, ready for it to discharge with the next surge in load. The operation of the system was smoothed electrically by careful adjustment of the boosters: motor-generator equipment which the sub-station operator would set to keep the Light Works load steady whilst slowly charging or discharging the battery.

Even so a busy afternoon could find the battery discharging at 200 amps one moment and charging at 150 amps the next, so the operator had to stay close to the switchboard in case an overload caused a circuit breaker to trip out: his aim was to put the switch back in before the trams on that particular section came to a stand, otherwise all the drivers would try to start at once and the heavy current might well pull the circuit breaker out again.

Figures for the summer of 1912 taken from electricity meters on the trams

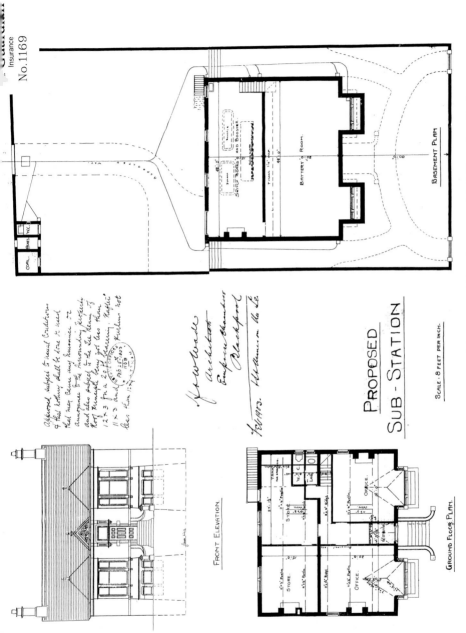

PROPOSED

SUB-STATION

SCALE: 8 FEET PER INCH.

BASEMENT PLAN

FRONT ELEVATION

GROUND FLOOR PLAN

Original drawings of the sub-station submitted to the Clifton Estate Offices for approval in 1903.   *Guardian Insurance*

Lytham bus No.3 (TC 5294) stands outside Squires Gate Depot in September 1923, when new.

Official photograph

Lytham St Annes No.35 was the first of the initial batch of tram replacement buses bought in 1936. It is seen in a later livery in Clifton Square, Lytham, in the 1950s. *R. Marshall*

show that the little open-toppers used approximately 0.7 units of electricity for each mile run.

Early Buses

The Tramways Company had operated a red 34hp Daimler char-a-banc on long distance tours even as far as the Lake District from August 1913, to September 1914, when it was requisitioned. The 'Blue' buses of modern times can be said to have their beginnings in two vehicles which entered service on Monday 6th August, 1923, on a route from St Annes Pier to Clifton Square, Lytham, avoiding the direct tram route. These were No.1 (TC 4897) and No.2 (TC 4898), Guy B types with front-entrance 20-seat Blackburn Aero Co. bodies. They cost £1,000 each and were worked by one man. By June 1924, a further seven of this type of bus had entered service, and on Friday 23rd July, 1926, buses replaced the tramway from Clifton Square to the Cottage Hospital. By this time there were a total of 13 buses in traffic, and several local sevices had been started within the Borough.

Tram Replacement Buses

When the section of tramway from Lytham to St Annes Square closed on Tuesday 15th December, 1936, the trams were replaced by the first double-deckers in the fleet. These were five Leyland TD4Cs with Leyland FH30/24R bodies, Nos.35-39 (BTB 929/930, BTC 621-623). They entered service between October and December of 1936. Another five Leyland TD4Cs entered service in March 1937, Nos.45-49 (BTF 25-29), and these replaced the trams after the last section of tramway closed on 28th April, 1937. The last of the tram replacement buses was withdrawn in 1964 after 27 years in traffic.

This is a picturesque view of Clifton Street, Lytham, with two trams of the Blackpool, St Annes & Lytham Tramways Company - No.16 in the foreground is waiting to depart for St Annes and Blackpool, whilst No.11 behind is about to disappear down Clifton Street on its way to East Beach. *TD Collection*

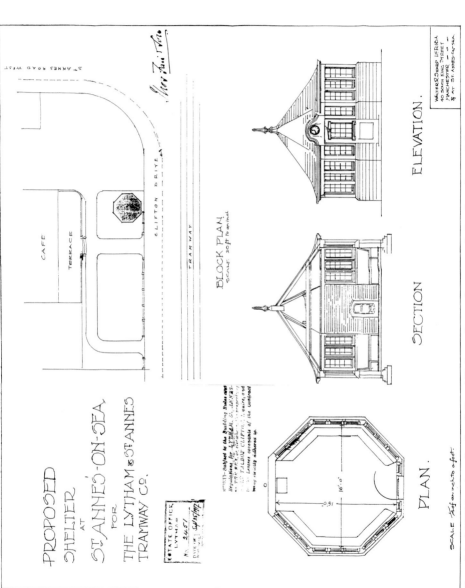

The original 1917 drawings for the shelter at St Annes Square (now extended and used as an information centre).

Guardian Insurance

Mishaps

Top: No.5 stands in the depot yard at Squires Gate in Company days awaiting transfer to the workshops after an accident.
Ted Lightbown, Blackpool Historical Society

Centre: The debris of a sandstorm has derailed No.41 and grounded it in the sandhills along Clifton Drive North *c.* 1935   *IM Collection*

Right: Another view of the same incident.
JG Collection

The End of the Trams

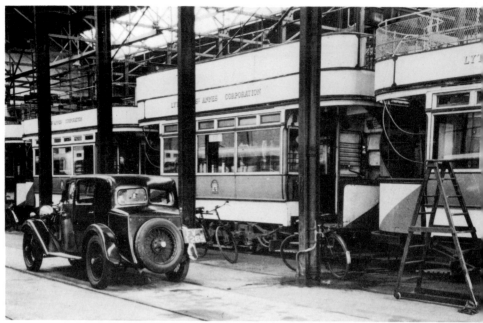

Four of the original BEC cars, *left to right*, Nos. 8, 3, 15 with 21E truck and extra panelling to the top deck, and No.1, seen here on 8th April, 1937.   *H.B. Priestley*

Pullman cars Nos.46 and 44 are framed by the staging for washing top decks the same day.
H.B. Priestley

The dismantling of Pullman car No.45 has apparently commenced, with the body being jacked up clear of the Peckham P22 truck. Note the straight spur gear through which each axle was driven, and the sand pipe dangling down from the body. *H.B. Priestley*

The pile of woodwork in the foreground bodes ill for these trams at the back of the depot in 1937 (No.35 at the right). *F.Deane/NTM*

Appendix One

Crossing the Ribble
by A. Winstan Bond

(Reproduced with permission from the July 1969, issue of *Modern Tramway*)

This is an account of romance blighted, a tale of marriage unfulfilled. The scene is the mouth of the Ribble, the lovers the tramways of Southport and Lytham, and the result the maddest tramway never to be built. Even today there is no direct link between Southport and Lytham, so a journey which could be cut to seven miles demands 31 miles via the nearest road crossing at Preston. If motorists are impatient today, tramway promoters were equally so. Why, on a clear day you could see Blackpool Tower from Southport. At low tide, the foolhardy even attempted to walk across the sands.

In October 1896, the aptly-named S. Speedy, architect, of Southport, publicly presented a plan to connect the Southport and Lytham tramways, crossing the Ribble by a swing bridge. Meetings were held and a committee formed but the scheme died within months.

Two years later, another hopeful appeared on the scene - J.T. Wood of Liverpool. His idea proposed a different solution for each stage of the journey. At Southport, a conventional tramway would branch off the Albert Road track, run up Park Road towards the Promenade, where it would turn on to the sea cop, and across Hesketh and Scarisbrick estates. All this line was to be on private right of way through marshland. Before reaching the estuary, Crossens sluice would be spanned by a viaduct 4.40 chains in length.

Beyond this point, the tramway would take to sea. Brighton and Magnus Volk had shown the way a few months earlier with the Brighton-Rottingdean 'Daddy-Long-Legs'. Volk's sea-going tram had four long legs to support the body. At the base of each leg was a 2 ft 8½ in gauge truck designed to run on one of two parallel tracks laid on the sea bed, which was exposed at low tide. The distance between the two outer rails was 18 ft. Extra tall standards curved at the top to support the trolley wire. By creeping forward at 6 miles/h tides of 15 feet were negotiated. This cross between a tram and a pier was adopted by Wood, who suggested that a similar railed sea-going vehicle met all trams and carried them, with passengers promenading outside the car, to a point near the channel of the River Ribble.

Here, so that there would be no interference with navigation, the tramcar would run off the platform and on to a transporter bridge for the mid-channel journey. The deposited plans preserved in Southport Library do not extend to this point but we have attempted to portray the probable layout of the estuarial transfer station in the accompanying drawing. Contact with Lytham would be finalised by a private pier from East Beach out towards the north side of the channel, where the transporter bridge ended. A further length of track via East Beach to Lytham (Market Square) would complete the connexion with the Lytham tramways (then gas-operated) and create a line 36 miles in length from Southport to Fleetwood.

The Southport and Lytham Tramroad Bill was presented to Parliament in time for the 1899 Session. The estimated cost of the line was £300,000, but the *Electrical Review* did not think the scheme too bold. After all, the 'brilliant and locally-unlooked-for financial success of the Blackpool and Fleetwood Electric Tramroad Company furnishes an example of the results which follow the paths of enterprise, and an incentive to disregard gloomy foreboding.' It was just a matter of time before Liverpool was connected by tram - 'and a short time only' - and here rapidly falling before the editorial pen were Lancaster, Morecambe, Lake Windermere, Rhyl, Llandudno and Bangor.

But there was a problem. 'Preston had crippled its financial resources for a generation in a vain endeavour to become a seaport, and anything which threatens to silt up or in any way interfere with its already too shallow navigable highway is sure to meet with some determined and undoubtedly successful opposition.' Lytham and St Annes could also be expected to oppose, as any further silting up of the estuary would result in the beaches at those places looking even more like Southport at low tide. Southport Town Council gave the scheme their blessing, a company was formed, and in June 1899 the House of Lords considered the Bill.

As anticipated Preston attacked in defence of her shipping interests. Mr Balfour Brown QC, appeared for the promoters. After mentioning that the platform tram would run for two and a half miles between the marsh and the start of the transporter bridge, he observed that though the latter feature was included to placate Preston, 'he was sorry to say that the docks there were still nearly empty.' However if Preston did not thrive it could not be the fault of this Bill. A working model of the transporter bridge was produced. The real thing would be 980 feet from tower to tower, and 103 feet above high water level, with its carriage suspended eight feet above wave level.

Argument centred on two points: could shipping clear the bridge, and would the scheme silt up the channel? Sir G. Pilkington MP, called for the promoters, said that there was no ship that could not pass under the bridge by lowering its gallant mast, and there was nothing in the scheme calculated to cause accretion. Other favourable evidence included that of the Mayor of Southport and Captain S. Nowell, consulting naval expert and marine surveyor who 'had taken measurements of considerably the largest sailing vessel that had gone to the port during the last 15 months and found that by striking her top gallant mast, which was a simple operation, she could pass under the bridge with something to spare.' A London firm of iron merchants spoke glowingly of the Bilbao transporter bridge, while R. G. Moore, M.Inst.C.E., the joint engineer for the scheme, offered to raise the height of the bridge to 150 feet above water level, even though this would cost an additional £12,000. This concluded the case for the promoters.

Preston Corporation called A. F. Fowler, resident engineer in charge of the Ribble Navigation Works. After pointing out that the bulk of the trade to Preston was by sailing vessel, he demanded a height for the transporter bridge of not less than 200 feet above wave level, as there were many vessels with masts as high as 187 feet. Captain Vereker, RN, of the Fisheries and Harbours Department of the Board of Trade was called. He was acquainted with the conditions, and urged caution. He had been working on the assumption that the platform tram was to run on an embankment, however, now that he was informed that the rails were to be laid flush with the sands he did not view this part of the scheme with the same apprehension. Two Trinity House pilots had a good moan, and were followed by Mr Pember QC, representing Preston Corporation who 'had doubts whether any large number of persons would desire to be conveyed in cars pendulum-wise over this windy estuary with a chance of being made sea-sick on the way. The scheme was defeated, except for the line from Southport to the edge of the marsh, for which there was no opposition.

The Southport and Lytham Tramroad Company were not to be put off, and in 1900 presented a further Bill. The platform tramway was abandoned, and instead the Southport tracks would follow the coast for a further three and a half miles to the site of an old ford. Here an iron pier, seven furlongs 4.10 chains long, would stretch out to a redesigned transporter bridge. In evidence, J.T. Wood said that the pier and bridge would cater for wagons, animals and merchandise as well as tramcars. For this purpose the carriage, or cradle would be 50-60 feet long, support 25 tons and take 1½ minutes to cross the channel. The motorman would be on a small upper deck, and would have the same control of the cradle as an ordinary electric tramcar under its driver. The cradle was to hang from 130 feet long rods, but 'there could never be a pendulum motion.'

As to the danger of hitting a vessel well, there was no traffic to interfere with, statistics

showing that only 1.75 ships (the fractional part presumably sinking fast) navigated the Ribble per tide. The total cost was estimated at £183,500, including £53,154 for the transporter. Sir George Pilkington, MP, the Mayor of Southport and others supported. For the opponents of the Bill, Preston's resident engineer kept harping on the money that Preston had sunk in the Ribble. Perhaps if the company would take up his suggestion of a tunnel, the 'sentimental' objections of master mariners would disappear.

This time, the company won their case and the Bill was passed. The Lytham tramways, for their part, built a 1,100-yard extension from the Market Square along Clifton Street and Warton Street to East Beach, where the line to Southport would now commence, and another company was actively promoting a tram road from Lytham to Preston. In 1902, the Southport & Lytham company obtained an extension of time to make up for the delay occasioned by 'the war'. Meanwhile, the newly-electrified Lytham tramways had instituted through bookings with steamers plying between Lytham and Southport. Negotiations between the Southport-Lytham and Preston-Lytham promoters gave rise to possible through running from Southport to Preston but after some lawyers were a little richer the Preston and Lytham Tramroads Bill was rejected by the House of Lords and nothing more was heard.

The next move was also off stage, but not without significance. The transporter bridge between Widnes and Runcorn was completed, J.T. Wood being joint engineer. This was the first such bridge in Britain, though earlier specimens existed abroad, and bright developments were now forecast at the Ribble. Sir Hiram Maxim was quoted as the chief supporter of the scheme, and his firm of Vickers, Sons and Maxim were awarded the contract in 1904 and had agreed to take 25 per cent of the contract price in shares. In August, work on the transporter bridge was said to be about to start.

However, 1904 gave way to 1906, the only activity being the passing of the .Southport and Lytham Tramroad (Extension of Time) Bill in May 1906. Southport had commenced by opposing the Bill, as the inactivity of the promoters was hindering the development of the town. The company countered, claiming to have already spent £40,000, all of which would be lost unless they went on. Opposition was withdrawn on the understanding that the embankment should be completed by December 1907 and the tramway, so far as it was on Corporation land, by July 1908, but capital was not forthcoming, and the powers expired unexercised in 1910.

The next scheme was mooted before the remains of the last could have been decently forgotten. In 1912, Mr Mallins, the Liverpool tramway manager, was asked to outline a plan for the development of the area's tramways, and proposed a line to Ainsdale which could eventually form a link in a chain from Liverpool to Blackpool via the Ribble estuary.

Between the two World Wars, several further schemes for crossing the Ribble, mainly by road, appeared, ranging from a tunnel in 1935 to a 42 ft high dam in 1938. The most intriguing ideas were those of George Bennie, the inventor of the 'Railplane'. In 1927 he proposed his propeller-driven 'monorail' for a 21-mile line from the Hesketh Bank to Lytham. The monorail structure would cater for ordinary track on an upper deck. The central span was to be 600 feet long, give an 85 foot clearance above high water and be approached by 1 in 50 gradients. Costs were estimated at £750,000. Preston was not impressed, and required a clearance of 181 feet, but Blackpool was very interested and offered to back a 1930 plan for a Bennie Railplane from Fleetwood via Blackpool, Kirkham, Hundred End, Southport, and on to Liverpool and Manchester. Needless to say, nothing resulted though Bennie was perhaps consoled for a while by his demonstration line at Glasgow.

So, perhaps, ended the quest for a tram across the Ribble. If only the promoters had raised the money to build their line in its 1900-1906 form, they would have found themselves in charge of a first-rate asset, a toll-earning bridge across the Ribble estuary used in ever-increasing numbers by motorists to avoid the long detour and the traffic-

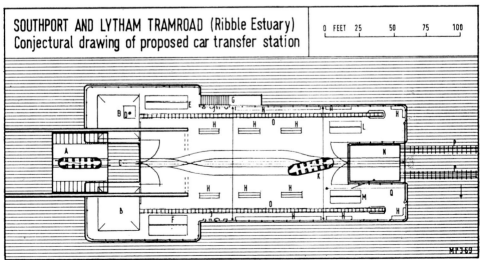

SOUTHPORT AND LYTHAM TRAMROAD (Ribble Estuary)
Conjectural drawing of proposed car transfer station

0 FEET 25 50 75 100

Legend: A—transporter arriving from Lytham; *B*—bridge towers; *C*—bay for transporter car; *D*—feeder pillar; *E*—staff offices; *F*—refreshments; *G*—stairs; *H*—seats; *J*—vending machines; *K*—Lytham-bound car leaving Volks-type platform; *L* and *M*—toilets; *N*—Volks-type platform car; *O*—bridge chains; *P*—twin underwater tracks; *Q*—overhead contact wire for Volks-type car.

jams of Preston. A Blackpool railcoach crossing to Southport would have made a novel postcard to send home and, although they never reached Southport, something very similar did appear on Southport's own pier tramway; but that is another story.

The author wishes to record his thanks to Southport Borough Library for their assistance in locating details of the Tramroad scheme and for taking tracings of the deposited plans, and to Mark Pearson of Leicester for preparing the excellent illustrations.

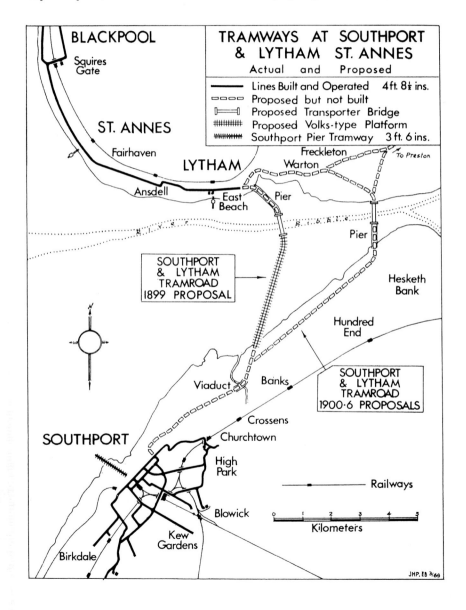

Appendix Two

Blackpool to Preston by Tram

The *Blackpool Times* (27th March, 1901) says:

In these dull days one matter alone seems to carry with it success. Whatever pays or does not pay, a Tramway pays when it has half a chance.

The success of the Blackpool and Fleetwood System is too well known to need comment. The shares are now at £4 premium, and the Blackpool Corporation Trams have been a great success, and have contributed materially to the relief of rates.

We are given to understand that the success of the Corporation Trams this year has been remarkable. Hearing reports and whispers and rumours of the projected sale of the Blackpool and Lytham Tram System to a Syndicate, and hearing also that this purchase was being made with a view to a light railway at least as far as Preston, a representative of the *Times* sought out a gentleman who was said to be staying in the town for the purpose of considering a light railway scheme.

With some difficulty our representative ran Mr Engineer down, and soon had him talking on Electric Traction in general, and then by insensible stages he was induced to talk of further extensions and developments.

> The Corporation Tram report, following upon the Fleetwood success, will make us all look around for other worlds to conquer. Its swift cars, its punctual service, and delightful ride show a handsome dividend for a capital of nearly £200,000. Its shares usually stand at 50 per cent premium. Small wonder that Lancashire and Blackpool investors are looking after similar good projects.

'Well what about the Blackpool and Lytham Trams?'

The Blackpool-Lytham route, we have said, is a superior one to the Fleetwood route. The whole town is moving in that direction, namely, southerly.

Soon the streets of houses which are running up with lightning rapidity will extend along most of the seven miles. The Electric Tramway is urgently called for. The importance of such towns as St Annes-on-the-Sea, preferred by tens of thousands of the quiet kind of visitors, and the town of Lytham, with its beautiful park, demands that the perfect and swift line of Blackpool Electric Tramways should continue right on. the present Company, under its previous Acts of Parliament, has the right to through bookings from the North Pier at Blackpool.

This resulted at once in such swarms of passengers congregating at the terminus that the management besought the town to discontinue it! The fight for the solitary car, coming once in very twenty minutes, was so fierce and the language too awful for any self-respecting conductor to listen to.

So the poor old single-line Tramway returned to its old ways in peace.

Sale of the Blackpool, St Annes and Lytham Tramways

And so the longed for and inevitable has come at last! The line has been purchased, at least so the secretary's circular announces. More popular news to Blackpool people it would be difficult to conceive.

Tens of thousands of Tramway passengers have longed for this consumation for years. The welcome intelligence is that the line will be doubled without delay. It will be equipped with all that the latest improved electrical plant can do. The cars are to be a revelation of luxury and elegance, and, still greater news - the line is to be continued to Preston.

The Preston Line

The Blackpool, St Annes and Lytham Trams already travel nearly half way to the great town. But what does this mean? A change for Blackpool when connected to Preston by Trams is certain.

When 120,000 population, or perhaps nearer 130,000, are brought nearer by Tramways, and swift Electric cars run every few minutes, the character of the whole town becomes affected. There will be more continuous, more steady, progress.

Property in the town will be affected, both here and along the route. What will it do for Preston? Preston will soon begin to live at the seaside. A few minutes' run by tram, and the beautiful meadows of Freckleton and the shores of the Ribble will be reached. Such places as Freckleton, Lytham, and the other places along the route will become increasingly important.

Compare the Fleetwood line with such a comparatively insignificant town as the terminus, and nothing on the way, with the new Tramway, having no less a town than Preston, with its factories, docks, and tens of thousands of operatives and workpeople at one end, and no less a town than Blackpool at the other.

The Block at Preston

The Lancashire millions come this way to Blackpool, that is, via Preston. What more natural than that after being done to death in a cramped up, dusty and sultry railway carriage for several hours, and having to wait with the line blocked, as they often do at Preston, they should alight and take a far cooler and more delightful ride on top of the tram along the coast? We can here the cry, 'Change here for Blackpool Tramways, and save two hours' wait.' Let the new Company understand we expect them to make this Preston-Lytham-Blackpool line the best Blackpool Electric Tramway, and may they equip it worthy of such a name, for the convenience and pleasure of the inhabitants and the millions of excursionists alike.

'But what about the new Company - the financial arrangements?'

'Well, we propose to call it the "Blackpool Electric Tramways Company - South," or some such name. And I may also say that in undertaking this scheme, the constructors are returning to the scene of their former triumphs. It was the same company whose engineers designed the original conduit line on Blackpool Promenade.'

'So confident are the promoters that they will rely for their profits partly upon the premiums and shares.'

'That's a fairly good test of your own confidence in the scheme, at any rate.'

'Well the premiums make a very substantial sum. You see, £4 premium on the present Blackpool and Fleetwood Tramroad, and our line has towns and streets which they have not.'

'How can shares be obtained?'

'They are being bespoke now. Part of the capital was guaranteed before we made the offer to buy up the Blackpool, St Annes, and Lytham tramway.'

'The old shareholders also are in many cases making it a condition that they shall be paid in the new Electric Tramway Company shares. In short, they refuse the money. A Blackpool Tramway is not to be got every day, especially when everyone knows how they are swarmed with passengers during the season. Besides, this new Company will be a rich Company, being owner of a great deal of land in a most promising district. It may create new suburban towns near Preston. All Preston wants to live a little way out in a more delightful neighbourhood, for you must admit Preston itself is dirty enough. The air across the meadows at Freckleton is lovely.'

Growth of Blackpool and District

'Yes. We are encouraged by the phenomenal growth of Blackpool and the general prosperity of Lancashire. Blackpool has grown in population from 23,000 at the last census to over 50,000, which, I believe, is the figure you expect to score on Sunday next when the census is taken.'

'That is so,' said our representative. 'there will be some disappointment in Blackpool if we don't reach over that magic 50,000. You see, we want to be a County Borough,' etc.

'What is your estimate of the number of visitors to Blackpool?' inquired the Engineer.

'Well, various estimates have been made, but certainly between three and four millions, and probably nearer four than three, in the course of one year.'

'These are wonderful figures,' he said. 'I can assure you that the promoters of this line know their way about. Such figures as you give encourage us; the success of your own Corporation Trams, the success of the Blackpool and Fleetwood Tramroad Company, which, in our opinion, will not have half the chances and opportunities for successful work of this line, and the success of other ventures. I may say also that we shall run goods - light goods perhaps - on the Tramways at night, and we will make it the best line in England, both for comfortable running, quick, frequent and punctual service, and for the internal luxuries of the cars, which will have more looking glasses, velvet, and soft cushions than any cars in England. In fact, we will beat your Corporation trams.'

'And when are you going to start?'

'At once; and I may tell you the policy will be very different to that of the old company. We shall meet the wishes of your Corporation in every possible way, and go out of our way to please them in all matters.'

Proceeding, the Engineer remarked:

The Tramway traction investments keep up in these dull times better than any other investment. The roadway, remember, is the most valuable part of the land. In buying the Blackpool and Lytham line we shall, of course, rely chiefly upon the rights conferred by the Act of Parliament; we shall sweep away the present plan and put in the newest and best, as I have said before, and we have no doubt of the ultimate, nay, immediate, success of the scheme.

'But is this the full extent of your ideas?' asked the Pressman.

'No,' was the answer. 'We have other schemes ahead still. This Blackpool-Lytham section is but the terminus of a great scheme for electric traction right through to Preston and then further on to Blackburn, Burnley, Colne, and East Lancashire.'

'So that it will be possible,' said our representative, 'to revive the old coaching days, and ride on the top of a Tram from Colne to Blackpool?'

'That is the idea,' said he, 'and you won't be much longer, I hope, before you have that ride.'

The above scheme is a literal realisation of the prophecy made in these columns at the time the Lytham and St Annes Tramway undertaking was being matured. 'Though we have no present knowledge of any further extraordinary extension of Tramway facilities,' we wrote at the time, 'all the indications point to a connection being made to Preston in the near future. such a large population as that of the Proud Town is sure to be tapped sooner or later, and it is not too much to say that the present generation may live to see a continuous tramway service from Preston, along the Blackpool front, to the Wyre Port.' How near that prophecy is of being fulfilled is easily seen.

The *Manchester Chronicle* (March 28th, 1901), says:

It is good news to Blackpool to learn that the statement to the effect that the Lytham and St Annes Tramway Company's undertaking has been acquired by a Syndicate, who are about to seek powers to construct a Tramway from Preston to Blackpool, where it will join the system now running to Blackpool, turns out to be true. It is claimed for the Blackpool Corporation Electric that they were the first, not only in England, but in the world; their success is almost too well known to need comment. Hundreds of visitors to the sea coast pleasure resorts have made good use of the cars at their disposal, and the profits have been high.

The new undertaking will be a large one, and the capital of the new Company will be £350,000. The line is to be doubled without delay, and will be equipped with all the latest improvements. the track is to be extended to Preston, to which town the Blackpool, St Annes, and Lytham Trams already travel nearly halfway. The consummation of this scheme will be of immense benefit to Preston; in fact, the whole district within the influence of the new extension will be enriched. One effect of the new line to Preston will be that many journeying to Blackpool and its sister resorts will be able to alight at Preston and reach their destinations by the Electric Cars.

The present Blackpool-Lytham line has about a mile further to construct. This will be finished and then the road will go on to Freckleton, and thence, as a light railway to Preston. It is expected that the whole country side will be opened up *en route*. The phenominal [*sic*] growth of Blackpool, and the general prosperity of Lancashire are happy auguries for the success of the new scheme.

The *Blackpool Herald* (March 29th, 1901), says:

The converting of the Lytham and St Annes Tramway from the gas traction to the Electrical Overhead System is now assured. By almost insensible stages, the undertaking has passed under a new control. Instead of proceeding by the usual course of purchasing the company and its undertaking from its owners, the Electrical Syndicate has bought up something like three-fourths of the share capital at market prices, and so acquired control. The Company acquired powers last year to convert their line to an Electrical System by a special Act of Parliament, and this will enable the Syndicate to proceed with the work at once. It is the sanguine estimate of the promoters that Electrically driven Cars will be running between Blackpool and Lytham next Easter. This is within the range of possibility, for the Fleetwood line was commenced and finished within twelve months. The Company also propose to continue the line as a Light Railway from Lytham to Preston, but this section will be somewhat delayed, as powers will require to be obtained. Still, the securing of powers for Light Railway construction has been greatly simplified, and the scheme will be pushed forward as speedily as possible.

It is also understood that the Syndicate owns Tramways in the heart of Lancashire, and the suggestion is made that there will in the very near future be a direct connection with a network of lines connecting Blackpool with most of the great centres of population in mid, east and south Lancashire. There is even talk of an arrangement with the Southport-Lytham Company. This is in some sense a dream, but it is more than a dream when it is found to be built up on tangible operations now successfully going on.

The facts are few, they are easily absorbed, but the far-reaching meaning of this small group of facts is so considerable in extent that we are for the present content to suggest what it means to have ready and rapid facilities of locomotion of infinite value, first to the immediate locality, but also for those providing for those further afield, and all the whole influencing to a degree incalculable our material prosperity.

The New Syndicate's Objects

The great dream, in which we have all more or less indulged, of seeing the Fylde coast outlined with tramways, seems nearer realisation than ever, if all comes to pass that is now talked about.   The syndicate which has purchased the Blackpool-Lytham line consists wholly of outside gentlemen, who have been attracted to Blackpool like a good many more, with the belief that there is still a great future for the town.   The outsiders may eventually be joined by local men, but at present they are keeping everything to themselves. The old patchwork system of the antiquated horse and the unsatisfactory gas traction will be discarded entirely, and the overhead electric trolley method used. The cars, too, will be replaced by more up-to-date ones, which will be handsomely equipped. The stink of gas exchanged for fresh sea air, the oscillation of the car a forgotten item, and the speed of the trams of a swift and reliable character, the outlook for the Blackpool, St Annes, and Lytham tramway will, indeed, be rosy.

But the syndicate's scheme does not end here. they propose to finish the mile that has not yet been completed at the Lytham end, then go on to Freckleton, and thence to Preston, only in this neighbourhood the tramway will have been converted into a light railway. It is expected that much traffic of an agricultural character will be tapped along this portion of the line, whilst it is thought that much can be done in the way of securing excursionists to Blackpool, who, it is argued, would prefer the seaside trip in ease and comfort to the run along the railway in stuffy carriages. If all that is proposed becomes fact, then there will be a line of tramways and light railways all along the sea coast line and the north bank of the Ribble from as far as Fleetwood to Preston, a distance of over twenty miles.

Appendix Three

New Cars for Lytham St Annes Corporation Tramways

(Reproduced from the 20th March, 1924, issue of *Tramway & Railway World*)

The choice of a car for the Lytham and St Annes Corporation Tramways was a matter requiring serious consideration, owing to the physical conditions under which the system operates. The entire route of double track is laid parallel to the railway, and at no point is more than a quarter of a mile from it, while in some places it is practically adjacent. The railway fares are one halfpenny per mile on this route, and every inducement is offered to passengers by good service and comfortable travelling.

To compete with this service, the general manager, W.H. Laing, has designed a car for luxurious travelling, easy loading and unloading, and steady running. As will be seen from the accompanying illustrations, the car is of the single truck, top covered type, and its general dimensions are as follows - Length of car body over end pillars, 19 ft; length of platforms, 5 ft 7½ in.; and length of top cover, 19 ft. The weight of the complete car empty is 11 tons 6 cwt.

The seating is arranged so that the lower saloon has accommodation for 23 passengers, double seats being fitted on one side of a wide aisle and single seats on the other, with the end seat in each corner fixed longitudinally. This plan provides a wide entrance and exit space. The seats are of the Preston standard walk-over type, and are upholstered in rich brown art leather, and with spring seats and backs give the maximum comfort obtainable.

Interior decorations are carried out in teak with dark figured oak panels, harmonising with the art leather upholstering of the seats. The floor is covered with ¼ in. thick linoleum, and the roof decoration consists of bird's-eye maple veneer, panelled out with teak moulds in the main roof. The side of the roof is finished with a heavy cornice mould, so arranged as to form a ventilation chamber the full length of interior saloon and connected with special exhaust ventilator fittings placed below the roof of the lower saloon.

The upper saloon is of the standard tramcar type, the interior finish being similar to the lower saloon, i.e., teak mouldings and oak panels. The side windows are fitted with lazy tong balances, and are arranged to open the full length of the saloon.

The truck has a wheel base of 8 ft 6 in., and is fitted with Peckham pendulum gear on the axle boxes, which allows for lateral movement of the axles, and thus eases shocks to the car on curves.

Particular attention has been given to the springing of the truck to ensure a comfortably-riding car. The wheel diameters are 27 in., and in the design of the electrical equipment advantage has been taken of this. Two lightweight 32hp motors, rated at 500 volts, are used, giving a high free running speed to suit the service run by the existing cars. These motors give a clearance between the rail and gear case of 4½ in. Controllers are of the DB form, K3 type, fitted with notch regulators and run back preventer. A very even high acceleration is given, the notch regulators on the controllers preventing the usual jerky starting. Ten of these cars have been put into service, and they were supplied by the English Electric Company Limited, both the car bodies and electrical equipments being manufactured at their Preston works.

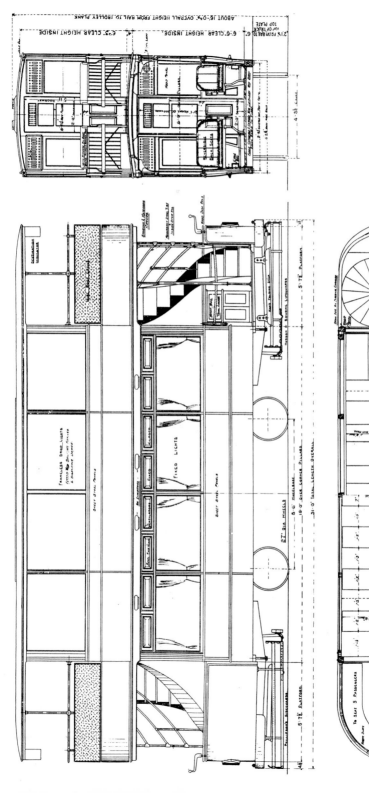

Elevations and Plan of New Car for Lytham St. Annes Corporation Tramways.

Acknowledgements and Bibliography

First a brief mention of the manner in which the three authors have divided the tasks involved in writing this history is appropriate.

Paul Abell   : research and text.
John Garnham   : specialist photography and research.
Ian McLoughlin   : research, text, maps and diagrams.

In addition many of the photographs used have come from the collections built up over the years by John Garnham (JG) and Ian McLoughlin (IM), by Terry Daniel (TD) - to whom special thanks, and also from the collection held by the National Tramway Museum at Crich, with particular thanks to Glynn Wilton. We owe a special debt of gratitude to Philip Groves for his detailed notes on the tram fleet, and also to the photographers who recorded Lytham trams in operation - it is very unfortunate that so many of their names have passed unrecorded, though naturally we have been very pleased to credit each photograph where we have been able to do so.

Our thanks are due to the following organisations and their staffs:

Blackpool Central Reference Library
Fylde Transport (formerly Lytham St Annes Transport Department)
Lancashire County Council Records Office, Preston,
Lytham St Annes Express, St Annes,
Lytham St Annes Libraries,
Manchester Central Library,
West Lancashire Light Railway, Hesketh Bank, near Preston.

We would also like to thank the following people who have contributed information and ideas which have helped us immensely: the late K.D. Burton, Frank Dean and Frank Dickinson; Winstan Bond, J.A. Cartmell, Ben Charlwood, Dougie Clarkson, Nicholas Entwistle, Dr Michael Harrison, Stuart Ibbotson; S.G. Lawrence, Scheme Manager, Neath Borough Council Training Agency; E. Lightbown, Blackpool Historical Society; Miss C.B. Lillystone, Archivist, Guardian Insurance; R.G. Manders, Museum of Science and Industry, Manchester; John Markham, Maurice O'Connor, Steve Palmer (posters), J.H. Price, Roy Scott, Jim Shearer, Marion Turner.

The Minutes and Accounts of St Annes Urban District Council and Lytham St Annes Borough Tramways Committees are held in the County Record Office at Preston, we have also referred to various issues of *Lytham St Annes Express*, Lytham St Annes Tramway staff magazines, *Lytham Times*, the *Blackpool Times*, *West Lancashire Evening Gazette*, the *Tramway & Railway World*, the *Railway World*.

The major published source is 'The Tramways of Lytham St Annes', by the late D.R. Phillips, in *Tramway Review* No.14 (1954), and more recently the tramway was included in *The Tramways of North Lancashire*, W.H. Bett & J.C. Gillham edited by J.H. Price, LRTA, 1985.

Other information illuminating various aspects of the history of the Lytham St Annes tramways may be found in the following published sources.

Lytham and St Annes: The Reluctant Resorts, Kath Brown, Lancashire County Books, 1992.
Rage of Sand: the Story of the Men who Built their Own Seaside Town, Gabriel Harrison, Ernest Benn, 1971.
The Blackpool Story, B.R. Turner & G.S. Palmer, 1976.
Blackpool to Fleetwood, B.R. Turner, LRTL, 1976.
Blackpool's Century of Trams, G.S. Palmer, Blackpool Borough Council, 1985.
Blackpool and Fleetwood By Tram, G.S. Palmer, Platform 5 Publishing, 1988.
'The Tramways of Preston', G.W. Heywood, *Tramway Review* Nos.69,70 (1972).
The Tramways of Accrington 1886-1932, R.W. Rush, LRTL, 1961.
Dearne District Light Railways, A.S. Denton, Omnibus Soc., 1980.
The Tramways of South Yorkshire & Humberside, W.H. Bett & J.C. Gillham edited by J.H. Price, LRTL, 1975.
The Tramways of South Wales, W.H. Bett & J.C. Gillham edited by J.H. Price, LRTA, 1993.
'Neath Corporation Tramways, 1897-1920', Gordon Tucker, *Tramway Review* Nos.107 and 108 (1981), with additional information in issues 127/9 of 1986/7.
'Gas Trams for Ipswich?', E. Gray, *Tramway Review*, Spring 1986.
Les Tramways Parisiens, Jean Robert, 2nd Edn 1969.
British Tramway Guide, P.H. Abell, AB Publishing, 4th Edn 1993.
The British Electric Car Company Ltd, J.H. Price, Nemo, 1976.
The Brush Electrical Engineering Company Limited & Its Tramcars, J.H. Price, Nemo, 1976.
The Evolution of the British Electric Tramcar Truck, A.M. Goodwyn, Nemo, 1977.

The lower deck of No.43 at Hesketh Bank on 10th November, 1985. The locomotive is Hunslet saddle-tank *Irish Mail*, built in 1903.   *John Garnham*